WHITE BELT
KEN図²KEN®
300 PUZZLES

CREATED BY
TETSUYA MIYAMOTO

**PUZZLE
WRIGHT
PRESS**

New York

CONTENTS

PUZZLE
WRIGHT
PRESS
New York

An Imprint of Sterling Publishing
1166 Avenue of the Americas
New York, NY 10036

Puzzlewright Press and the distinctive Puzzlewright Press logo
are registered trademarks of Sterling Publishing Co., Inc.

KenKen is a registered trademark of Nextoy, LLC

© 2013 by KenKen Puzzle LLC

ISBN 978-1-4549-0417-5

Distributed in Canada by Sterling Publishing
c/o Canadian Manda Group, 664 Annette Street
Toronto, Ontario, Canada M6S 2C8
Distributed in the United Kingdom by GMC Distribution Services
Castle Place, 166 High Street, Lewes, East Sussex, England BN7 1XU
Distributed in Australia by Capricorn Link (Australia) Pty. Ltd.
P.O. Box 704, Windsor, NSW 2756, Australia

For information about custom editions, special sales, and premium and
corporate purchases, please contact Sterling Special Sales at 800-805-5489 or
specialsales@sterlingpublishing.com.

Manufactured in Canada

4 6 8 10 9 7 5

www.puzzlewright.com

INTRODUCTION

KenKen is a fairly new puzzle. It was invented in 2004 by Tetsuya Miyamoto, a math teacher from Yokohama, Japan, as a tool to help improve his students' math and logic skills. He wanted something that would be entertaining enough to keep students interested, and, as it happened, he succeeded extremely well in creating something entertaining—people all over the world now solve and enjoy his invention daily.

KenKen, at first glance, may look a bit like sudoku. And, like sudoku, the rows and columns of a KenKen grid contain no repeated numbers. But that's where the similarities end. Here are the basic rules of KenKen:

- Fill the grid so that each row and column contains a complete set of digits, with no repeated digits in any row or column. (The set of numbers depends on the size of the grid; a 4×4 KenKen puzzle will use the numbers from 1 to 4, a 5×5 KenKen puzzle will use the numbers from 1 to 5, and so on.)
- Each heavily outlined box, known as a "cage," indicates a mathematical operation that must match the digits inside that cage. Numbers may repeat within a cage as long as they do not appear in the same row or column.

There are four mathematical operations that may appear in a KenKen puzzle. A plus sign indicates that the digits inside the cage add up to the given number, while a multiplication sign indicates that the given number is the product of the digits inside the cage. If a cage contains a minus sign, the given number is the difference between the digits in the cage (that is, the result of subtracting the smaller digit from the larger digit). In a cage with a division sign, the given number is the quotient of the digits in the cage (that is, the result of dividing the larger digit by the smaller digit). Cages with minus signs and division signs will never contain more than two digits. Single-cell cages contain no mathematical symbols, and simply indicate what digit they contain.

Now that you know the basics, let's turn the page and take a look at a sample puzzle, and solve it together.

First, we can fill in any 1×1 cages right away. There's one on the right side of the grid, and we can write a 1 in it. Below that is a rectangular cage with a quotient of 2. Since this is a 4×4 puzzle, which only uses the digits 1 through 4, that cage can only contain either the digits 1 and 2 ($2 \div 1 = 2$), or 2 and 4 ($4 \div 2 = 2$). Since that column already has a 1 in it, the correct pair must be 2 and 4, but we don't yet know which order they go in, so let's look elsewhere for more information. The 6+ clue on the bottom of the grid is helpful, because that's the lowest possible sum of three different digits ($1 + 2 + 3 = 6$); that means that cage must contain 1, 2, and 3. That accounts for three of the four digits in the row, so the remaining digit is a 4—which means we can now write the 2 in the other space of the 2÷ cage.

Other good places to look for information are in cages with high given numbers, which usually have fewer possible solutions. Take a look at the 16× cage. There are only two ways to make that product: $1 \times 4 \times 4 = 16$, or $2 \times 2 \times 4 = 16$. (In a larger puzzle, $1 \times 2 \times 8$ might be possible, but this grid contains no digits higher than 4.) Both of those solutions contain a pair of repeated digits, which must go in the two diagonally adjacent corners of that cage, so they don't share a row or column. But they can't both be 2's, since the third row already has a 2 in it, so they must be 4's, making the remaining cell in that cage a 1. And now the third row contains every digit but 3, so we can write that into the empty cell.

Whenever you write a digit in an empty cage, see if that new data helps solve that cage. In this case, we've just written a 3 into a 1− cage. That cage's digits must have a difference of 1, so they could be 2 and 3 ($3 - 2 = 1$) or 3 and 4 ($4 - 3 = 1$). But the second row already contains a 4, so the digit above the 3 must be 2. In fact, now that all but one 4 has been placed, only one possible square remains for the last 4, at the top of the third column. With that 4 written in, you should be able to easily complete that cage (and the rest of the puzzle). The solution appears upside-down at right.

Remember, every KenKen can be solved logically; you never need to guess to complete a puzzle. This book contains 300 easy puzzles: 50 4×4 KenKen, 150 5×5 KenKen, and 100 6×6 KenKen. Difficulty will increase gradually as you go. Happy solving!

1

2	12×		3−
2÷		3	
7+	3−		1−
	3+		

2

7+		3+	
3+		3	3−
3−	1−		
	2	7+	

5

3

10+		6+	1−
	3−		
3+		4+	7+
	2		

4

3+		10+	
2−	3−		
	2−		5+
7+			

6+	7+		2−
	2	3−	
4+			2−
3	3+		

2÷		12×	4×
3	6×		
4×		2÷	
	2÷		3

7

2÷		12×	
2÷	3	12×	2÷
3×		8×	

8

12×		24×	2÷
2÷	4×		
			12×
3	2÷		

12×		2÷	
2÷	4	3×	
	6×		2÷
3	4×		

4	3+		4+
2÷		6×	
2−	3		2÷
	3−		

4+	3−		2÷
	1−		
6×		3−	
3−		5+	

2÷		48×	3
2−	2		
	3−		2÷
7+		2	

3+	7+		1
	2	2−	2÷
1−			
3−		6×	

6+	6×		7+
	3−		
		12×	4+
2÷			

2÷	3−		2−
	1−		
12×		3	2÷
	3+		

2	3−	1−	
4+		6×	3−
	24×		
		2÷	

Puzzle 1 (4×4 grid):

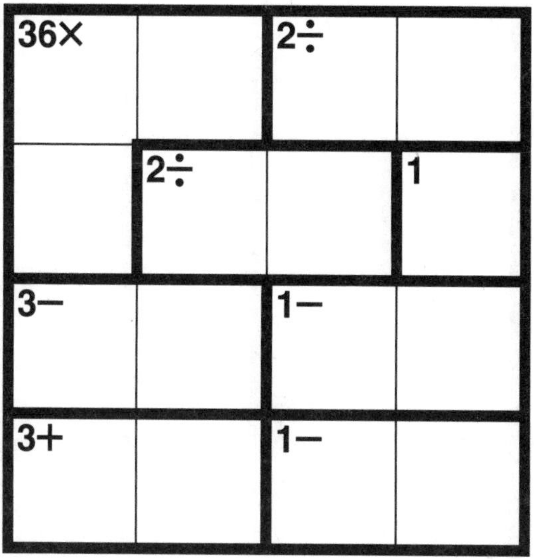 36×		2÷	
	2÷		1
3−		1−	
3+		1−	

Puzzle 2 (4×4 grid):

2÷	12×		2
	8+	6+	
			9+
3−			

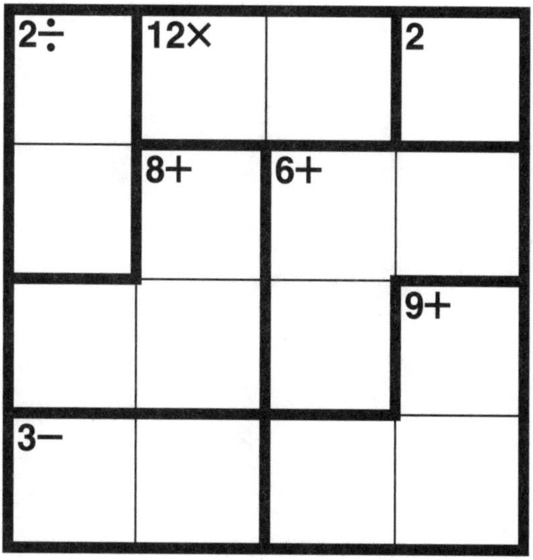

19

2÷		36×	
9+	2−	3−	
			2÷
	2÷		

20

2÷	2	4+	
	12×		3−
7+	2÷		
		2−	

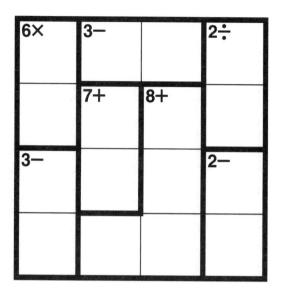

**2
1**

**2
2**

Puzzle 2/3

8×			1−
1−	3−	3	
		9+	2÷
1			

Puzzle 2/4

2÷	7+		1−
	8×		
1−		2÷	3−
	3		

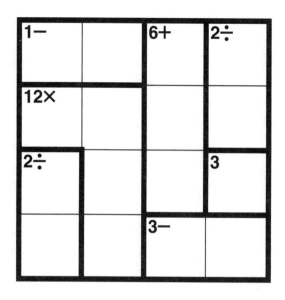

2/5

3− 24×

7+ 2÷

12× 4

5+

2/6

27

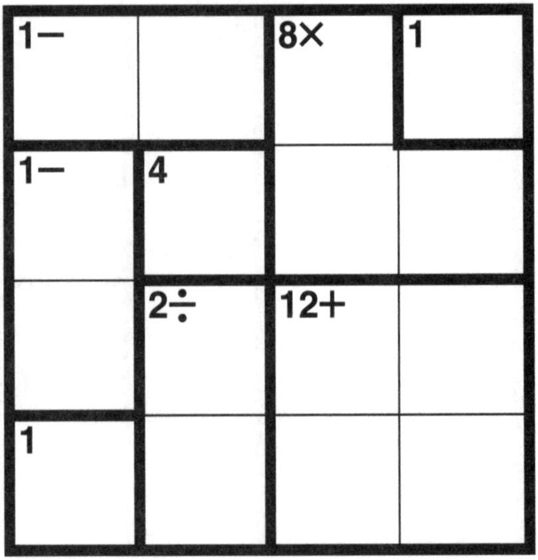

28

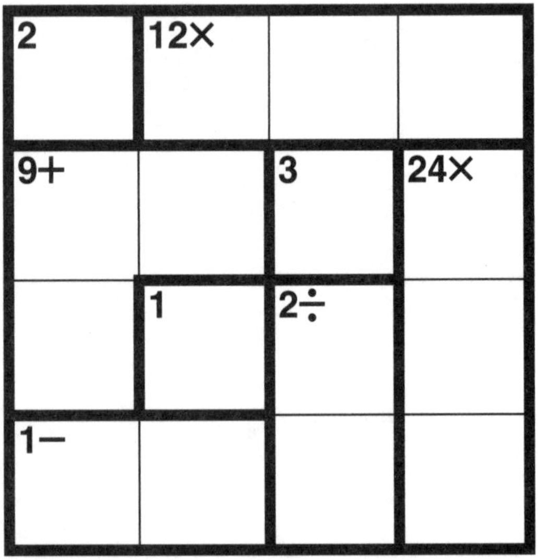

29

30

3+		48×	
8+	2		
	2÷		1−
	2−		

6+			1−
4	5+	12×	
2÷			
	1−		1

Puzzle 1

2÷		2−	3−
6×			
6+	1−		1−
		2	

Puzzle 2

12×			9+
2÷	4		
	1−		
3	8×		

3/3

3/4

6+	1−		2÷
	16×		
	8×		4+
		3	

4+		1−	
24×		2÷	
	3	12×	1−

Puzzle 3/7

7+		12×	2÷
2			
2÷		1−	1−
5+			

Puzzle 3/8

1−	6×	2÷	
		3−	
7+	3−		1−
		3	

Puzzle 39

12×	2÷		3−
	1−		
5+		12×	1−
1−			

Puzzle 40

7+		8×	
2÷			12×
2−	8+		
	1		

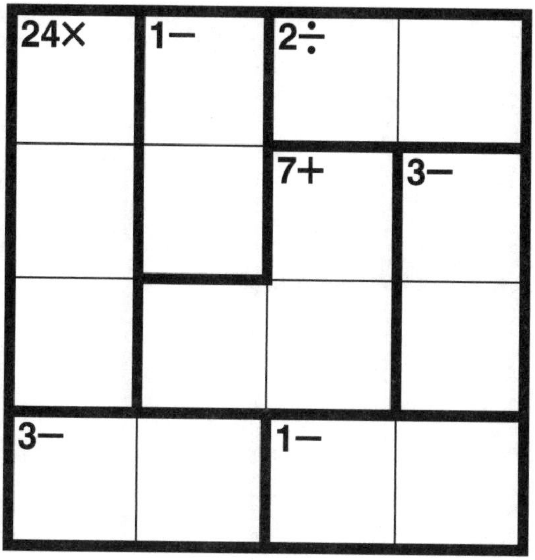
24×
1−
2÷
7+
3−
3−
1−

4
1

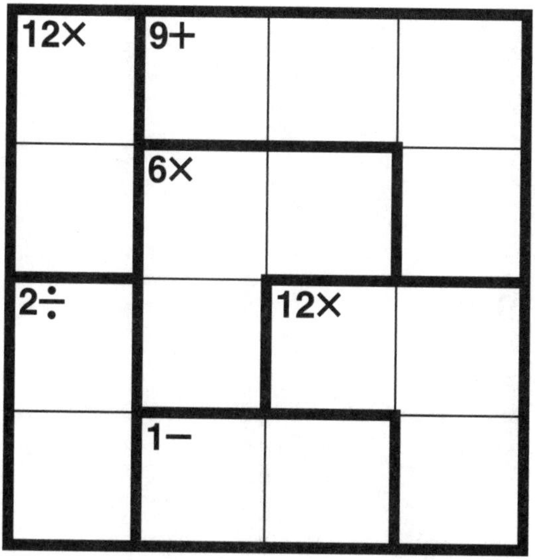
12×
9+
6×
2÷
12×
1−

4
2

2÷	1	36×	
			7+
2÷		1−	
1−			

2÷	24×	1−	
			1
9+		1−	
3		2÷	

Puzzle (top)

24×			1
3		2÷	
8+	1−		1−
		4	

Puzzle (bottom)

8×	3−		12+
	8+		2÷
1−			

4
7

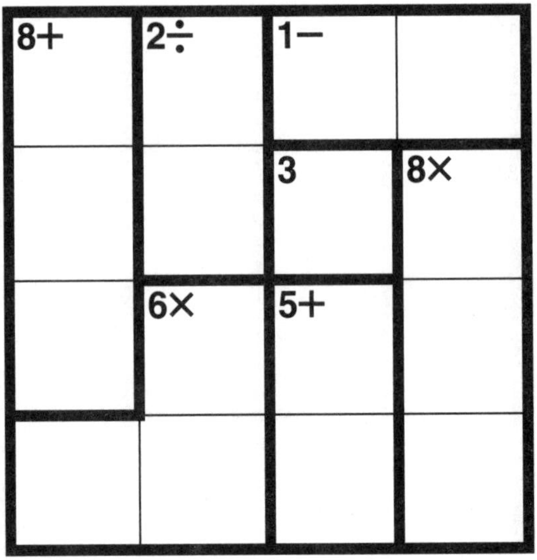

4
8

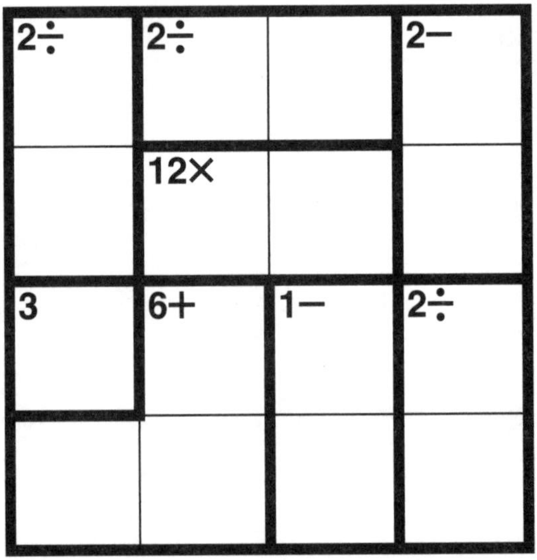

Puzzle 4 9

4+		2÷	
1−		1	1−
2−	2÷	12×	
			1

Puzzle 5 0

1	2÷		12×
10+			
		1−	
7+		2÷	

5 1

7+		8+	5+	
1−			6+	4−
4+	6+	3+		
			5	5+
4−		7+		

5 2

1−	3+		3	4−
	11+			
8+		7+		5+
3−		5		
3+		8+		4

8+		5	6+	
9+		3+		3
	2	8+	4−	
6+				3−
	9+		3	

5 / 3

9+	2	7+		5+
	9+	3+		
5+			8+	
	4−		2−	3−
4+		4		

5 / 4

5 / 5

15×		2÷		3×
2÷		5×		
12×	5	2÷		40×
	2÷	45×	4	

5 / 6

2÷		20×	3×	2×
3×	15×			
		6×	20×	
20×			2÷	15×
	2÷			

Puzzle 5/7

4×	15×		2÷	
	3	20×		12×
60×				
	2÷		80×	15×
2÷				

Puzzle 5/8

3×		80×		2÷
2÷	15×			
	5	6×	12×	
20×	2÷		2÷	15×
		1		

Puzzle 59

3+		30×		9+
2÷	4+		4−	
		4		6+
8+	4	9+		
	4−			

Puzzle 60

40×	1−	2÷	4−	
			1	18×
	4−			
4+		5	11+	
3+		12×		

Puzzle 6-1 (5×5 grid)

60×	4−	6×		5
		2÷		2÷
	12×			
2÷	9+		4+	
	6+		15×	

Puzzle 6-2 (5×5 grid)

1−		2÷	4−	
2−			2÷	2
3−	3+	9+		45×
3−		3	3−	

Puzzle 6/3 (5×5):

2÷	4−		1−	
	6×		14+	2
				10+
11+		2÷		
	2÷			

Puzzle 6/4 (5×5):

2−		2÷		40×
9+	12×			
	2÷		9+	2−
2÷		2		
	15×			

Puzzle 1 (top)

1−		10×		10+
2−	3+			
	5	16×		
2÷	24×			2−
		4−		

Puzzle 2 (bottom)

4−		11+		
2÷	15×			2−
	3−	7+	4−	
8+				20×
			3	

12×		2÷		40×
	4−	2−		
30×		2÷		
	2÷		7+	
	9+			1

1−		3+	20×	
9+	3−		4+	
		8+	4−	2÷
2−				
	1−		5+	

Puzzle 69

4−	9+		6×	
	1−	2÷		12+
2÷				
	36×		2÷	4−
		5		

Puzzle 70

2÷	9+	2−	4−	
			15×	1−
2÷		24×		
2−			3−	
	1	40×		

100×		2	6+	
1−			1	
2÷		9+		
3	4−		2−	
2÷		60×		

5	6×		2÷	
2−				12+
3+		4		
2÷	4−		1−	
	12×		4−	

7 / 3

4	3+		120×	
11+	4−			
		4	2÷	
2÷		9+		1−
3+			3	

7 / 4

3+		1−		4+
4	3−		1−	
12×				9+
4−	3	2÷		
	8+		2÷	

7/5

15×		2÷		1−
4	4−	24×		
6+			4−	5+
	2−	8+		
			3−	

7/6

2÷	10×		1−	
		13+		5+
4+			2÷	
8+	2−			10×
	8+			

Puzzle 7/7 (5×5)

4−	9+		6×	
	2−		12×	
1−		2÷	9+	
12×	4−			7+
		4+		

Puzzle 7/8 (5×5)

3−	6×		2	2−
		1−		
8+		2÷		4
9+		4−	24×	
1−				

Puzzle 79

12×		11+	4−	
	8+		5+	
			3	30×
4−	5+			
	2−		2÷	

Puzzle 80

10×		4−	11+	
2÷	30×		1	
			2−	
2−	5+	2−		3−
		2÷		

Puzzle 8/1:

2÷		2−		4−
30×	6×	3−		
			9+	3
	5+			2÷
15×			2	

Puzzle 8/2:

12×		30×		
	8×			9+
2÷	3−	4−	9×	
10+			5+	

45

8
3

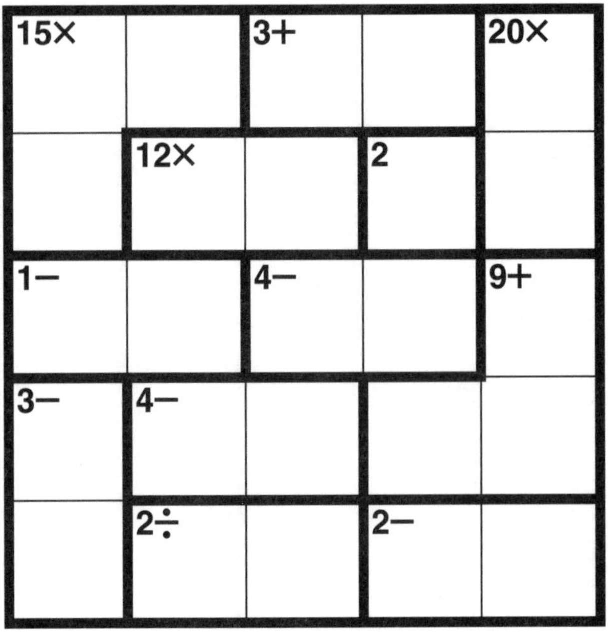
15×
3+
20×
12×
2
1−
4−
9+
3−
4−
2÷
2−

8
4

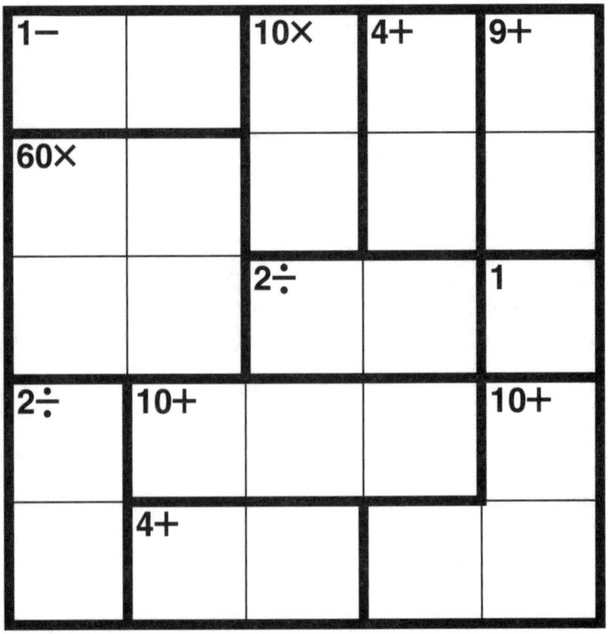
1−
10×
4+
9+
60×
2÷
1
2÷
10+
10+
4+

2÷		30×	2−	
3+			4	9+
	2−		9+	
8+	1−			5+
		4		

4−		48×	30×	
5+				
	2÷		1−	
3−	30×		4+	
		7+		4

8/7

1−		2÷	4−	
6+			60×	
12×	2÷	8+		1
			9+	
20×		3+		

8/8

3−		1−		4−
12×	3+	2÷	4−	
				3
6+	7+	5	2−	
		6+		

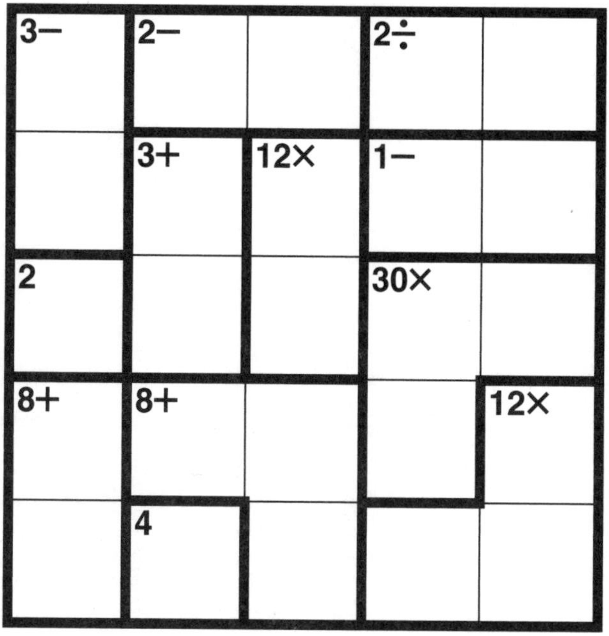

89

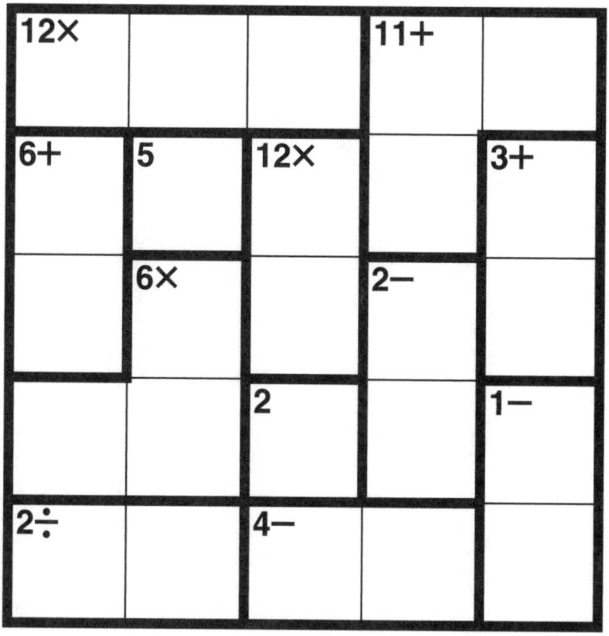

90

9/1

4−		16×	1−	
11+			8+	4−
9+	2−		2÷	
		2	3−	

9/2

2−		4	3−	
2÷	5	6+	1−	
	3+		4+	
2−		16×		4−
	1−			

Puzzle 9/3:

2−		40×		
2÷	30×		5+	
		4−		72×
15×	9+			
		3+		

Puzzle 9/4:

4−	3+		2÷	1−
	60×			
72×		8+	1−	
				4−
		9+		

Puzzle 1 (top grid):

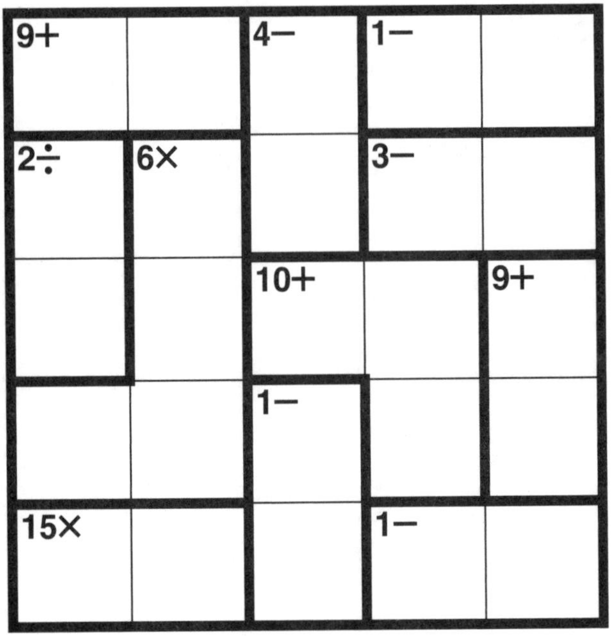 9+		4−	1−	
2÷	6×		3−	
		10+		9+
		1−		
15×			1−	

Puzzle 2 (bottom grid):

2÷		15×		7+
4−		6×		
1−	3		5+	30×
	2÷			
3		1−		

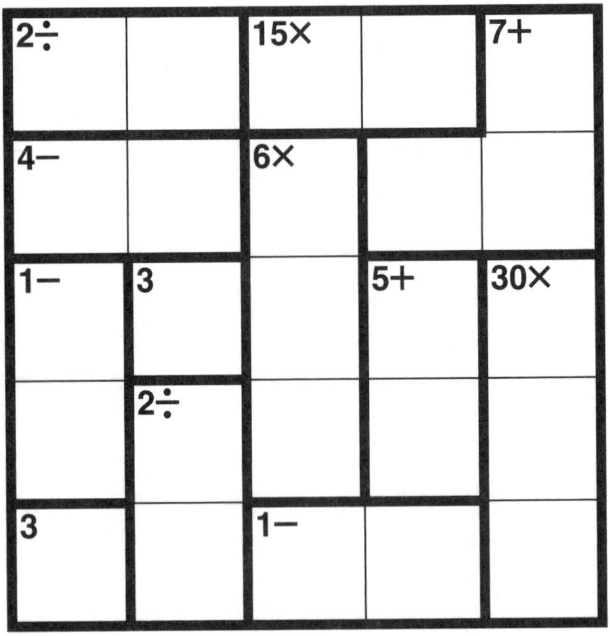

Puzzle 97 (5×5)

2÷	2−		1−	
	60×			9+
7+			4	
15×		2÷		
	2÷		9+	

Puzzle 98 (5×5)

2−	3+	60×	11+	
				4−
40×	1−		2	
		2÷		36×
	6+			

2−		4+		4−
90×		9+		
		2÷		11+
4−	12×			
	3−		1−	

5	2÷		1−	3−
2÷	2−	50×		
				6+
2−	20×			
	9+			5

Puzzle 101 (5×5 grid)

8×	2÷		8+	
		11+		2÷
300×			2÷	
5+		9+		4−

Puzzle 102 (5×5 grid)

2−		3+		1−
6+		20×		
	2÷		25×	
2−		3		2÷
4−		12×		

15×		3+		11+
2÷	4−			
	4+		8+	10×
3+		40×		
1−				

1−	3−	5+		3
		1−	4+	
2÷			4−	
9×	4−		8+	
		9+		

Puzzle 105

30×			9+	2−
3−				
7+	4−	3+	3	2÷
			50×	
12×				

Puzzle 106

2−	2÷	20×		2−
		2÷		
2÷	4−		60×	
	3×	7+		3−
			2	

12×	3−	2−		3+
		10×	7+	
5				9+
2÷	1−	2÷		
		4−		3

1−		4−		8×
30×			1	
3+	20×		12+	
	2÷			15×
4		5+		

1 0 9

20×	1	4−	7+	1−
	1−			
2÷		40×		
	2−		4−	5+
12×		2		

1 1 0

2÷		2−		48×
15×	5+			
	9+		3−	
	1−			4−
11+			3	

1
1
1

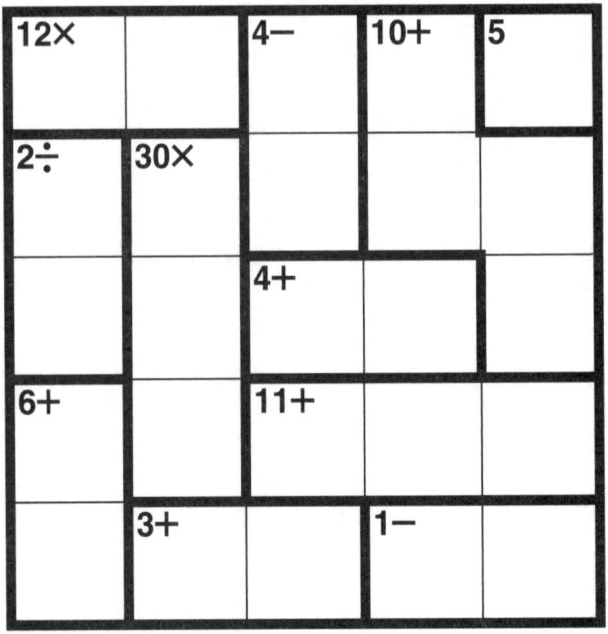
12×
4−
10+
5
2÷
30×
4+
6+
11+
3+
1−

1
1
2

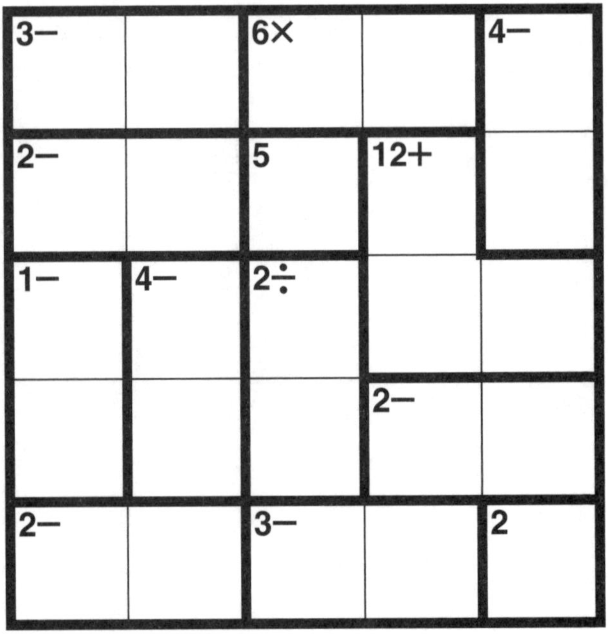
3−
6×
4−
2−
5
12+
1−
4−
2÷
2−
2−
3−
2

Puzzle 1:

9+		12×	7+	
2÷	4−			2−
			5+	
18×		7+		1
			1−	

Puzzle 2:

7+	60×		1−	
			4−	
4−		2÷	1−	
90×			9+	
		3−		2

Puzzle 115

10×	3+	1−		60×
		4−		
4+			3+	4
1−	2−			8+
	2÷			

Puzzle 116

6×		4−		12+
9+	3+			
	1−	7+	8+	
2÷				
	15×		3−	

117

4−		2÷	1−	
2÷	5		4+	6+
	24×			
7+		4−	1−	
			2÷	

118

24×		9+		2÷
	4−	15×		
4−		1−		12×
	7+			
1−			3−	

119

1−	1−	4−		2÷
		20×		
10×	9+	4+		2−
		4	1−	
	3+			4

120

2÷	1−		4−	
	10×		12×	
3		2÷		9+
8+			12×	
4−		4		

Puzzle 1

4−		2÷	4	6×
8+	3−			
		12+		
	4		10×	
30×				4

1
2
1

Puzzle 2

3	6+		50×	
13+			3+	
10×				8+
	2−			
2÷		60×		

1
2
2

1−	4−		2÷	
	15×		6×	
3−	10+			4
		2÷	4−	2−

1−	9+		10×	
	3×			2
2÷			11+	
1−		9+		
15×		2	5+	

2÷		4−		12×
1−	1−			
	3+		6×	9+
2−	15×			
	3−		3−	

9+	4+		24×	
	2÷			5
10×			24×	
1−	60×			
	4		4−	

2	2÷	2—		1—
9+		45×	2÷	
				6×
4—		2÷	20×	
2—				

1—		4—	8×	3—
3	3—			
5+		1—		8+
	2÷		6×	
9+		3		

Puzzle 129:

3+		36×		4−
2÷	20×			
	30×	6×		
2−			10+	
	5+			2

1 2 9

Puzzle 130:

5+	4+		10×	
	12+			2÷
10+	1−		4−	
	2÷			4+
	5	5+		

1 3 0

131

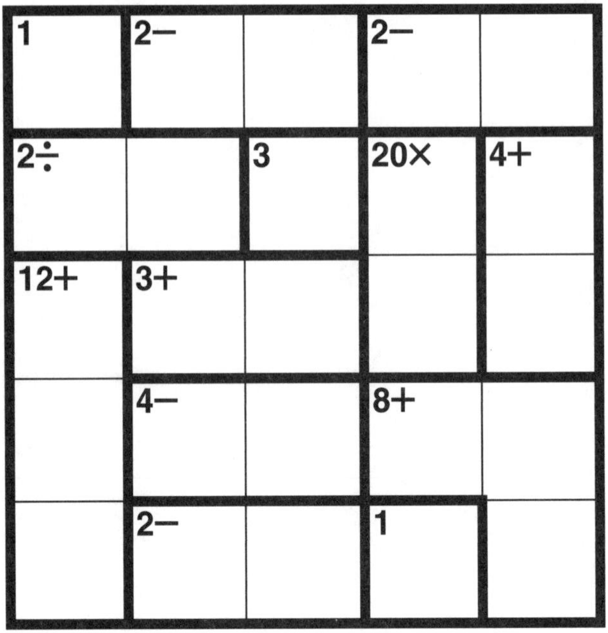
1
2–
2–
2÷
3
20×
4+
12+
3+
4–
8+
2–
1

132

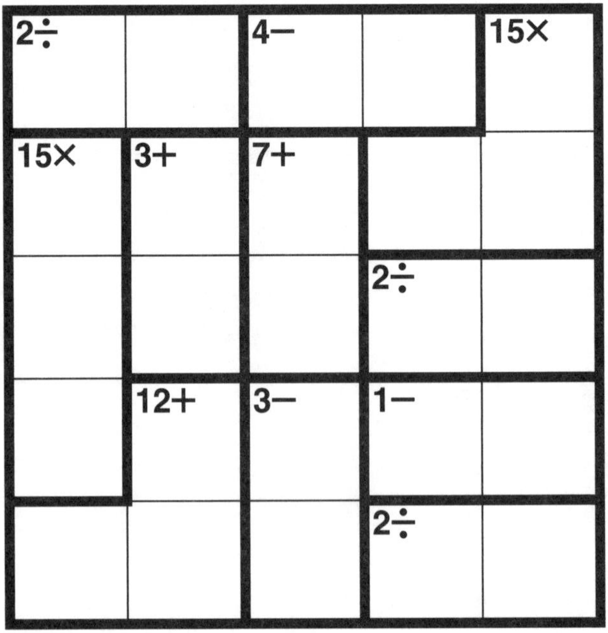
2÷
4–
15×
15×
3+
7+
2÷
12+
3–
1–
2÷

Puzzle 1 3 3

4−		2−	8×		
2÷			36×		
1−	2÷				
	11+	3+		50×	

Puzzle 1 3 4

2−		2÷		1	
3+	1−	12×			
		40×		1−	
12×	4−				
	5+		4−		

4+	1−		20×	
	2−		2÷	
15+			2−	
6+	3		15×	2÷
	4−			

4	2÷		2−	
3+	1−	4−	1−	
			6×	5+
8+	1−			
	7+		2÷	

137

2÷	60×		2÷	
		13+		
4+		2−		10+
200×			4+	
		1		

138

4−	15×	1−	2÷	
			3−	12×
4	3+			
48×		4−	2−	
			3−	

139

6×	20×	7+		7+
		2÷		
60×			5	2÷
	4+	2−	9+	

140

9+		6×	1−	6+
2÷				
2−	10×	20×		1−
		4−	4×	
1−				

74

Puzzle 1

15×	3+		1−	4
		3		10×
5+		6×		
3−	1−	2÷		4+
		4−		

Puzzle 2

4+		2−	2÷	
30×			3−	
	2÷		4−	
20×	3−	1−		2−
		2÷		

9+		10×		12×
2÷			6×	
4−	48×			
		10+		
3	2÷		1−	

1−	3−	9+	1−	
			2−	
2÷		30×	4−	
8+			16×	
	3	1−		

3−	6×		12+	
		1−		
10+	4−		24×	
	2÷		3×	
	9+			

1 4 5

2÷	40×			2−
	3	15×	2÷	
9+				4
	2÷		3	7+
2−		5+		

1 4 6

Puzzle 147 (5×5):

18×	4−		7+	1−
2÷		45×		30×
3−				
4−		2÷		

Puzzle 148 (5×5):

2÷	1	20×		10+
	1−		4−	
3	2−			
1−	8+	2÷	2÷	
			4+	

Top puzzle (1 4 9)

2÷	6×		2−	9+
	2−	3−		
4−			2÷	
	2÷		2−	
3	4−		2−	

Bottom puzzle (1 5 0)

3×		9+		10+
	2−			
2÷		4−		12×
10+		15×	2÷	

151

40×	3	15×	2−	
			6+	
1−			2÷	
3+		1−		3
4−		2	1−	

152

60×	1−		3+	4−
		5+		
4−	1−		2÷	
		3−	2−	
2÷			1−	

Puzzle 153

2÷		2÷	2−	
6+			1−	
40×	3	20×		
		2−		3−
12×		2÷		

Puzzle 154

1−	2÷	2−	1−	
			50×	2−
2−				
7+	9+	1−		2−
		2÷		

9+		2−	24×	
3−	5+		2÷	
		1−		15×
5+				
4+		40×		

48×		4−		2÷
	2÷	2−		
8+		8×	10+	4
	15×			
			1−	

157

10×	4−	1−		2−
		2÷		
2÷		11+	4−	40×
4				
1−		1−		

158

15×	2÷	1−		2÷
		6+		
6+			1−	
2÷		5+	1−	2−
9+				

2÷	2−		2−	1−
	1−	2		
5		12×		2−
2−	4	7+		
	9+		2÷	

1−	4−		18×	
	13+			5+
		2−		
2−	2÷		1−	
	12×		3−	

Puzzle 1

4+		60×	2÷	
3−				1−
30×	1−		6+	
		7+		3
			4+	

1
6
1

Puzzle 2

15×		2−		10+
9+		8+		
	1		90×	
2÷	60×			
		3−		

1
6
2

Puzzle 1-6-3

10×		7+	2−	1−
4−				
	5+	2−	2−	5
11+				2÷
		6+		

Puzzle 1-6-4

2−	3+		1−	
	12×	2	2−	2÷
12+				
		1−		2−
	4	4−		

Puzzle 165

3+		20×		2−
7+		2÷		
9+	1−		12×	
	1−			2÷
	3−		4	

1 6 5

Puzzle 166

9+		6×		1
1−	2÷		9+	1−
4−	2−		2÷	
	3−		1−	

1 6 6

Puzzle 167

4−	9+		1−	
	6×			2÷
10+		8+		
2÷			4−	
	3−		2−	

Puzzle 168

10+	2−		30×	
	2÷			9+
	32×		4−	
1−		2−		
	5		3−	

Puzzle 169

40×			1−	
3+		3−		8+
	2−		1−	
24×				2÷
20×		4+		

Puzzle 170

2−		2−	4−	
3−			1−	
5+		5	24×	
12+				7+
3	2÷			

171

2−		1−	50×	
30×	4			2÷
	6+			
		20×		
11+			2−	

172

1−		4−		5+
2−		8×		
2÷		5		1−
4−	5+	1−	30×	

Puzzle 173

4−		2÷		2−
2−	30×		1−	
				9+
2−	9+	4−		
			2÷	

Puzzle 174

2÷		2−		11+
6+	20×		30×	
	1			
	20×		9+	
2−				1

175

176

Puzzle 177

11+		3+		48×
		12+		
10+			3−	2÷
	6×			
		1−		5

Puzzle 178

4−	1−	40×		2−
			5+	
15×		2÷		9+
2÷	8+		10+	

11+	4−		12×	1−
	2−	10×		
4−		2÷		1−
	4	15×		

3−		12×		
1−	1−	15×	7+	
				2÷
7+	2−		2÷	
	2÷			5

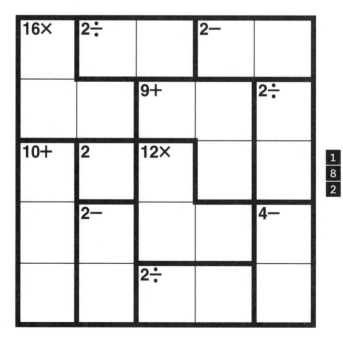

183

2−		2−		40×
1−	9+	4−		
			4+	
1−	2÷	4	15×	1−

184

40×		1−	7+	
			4−	
120×		2−		4
	10+	2÷		7+

60×	2−		3−	
		8+		3+
3−	9+			
	6×	2÷	1−	1−
1				

4−		16×	8+	
8+				4−
		1−		
3−	1−	2÷		1−
		2−		

187

2−	2÷	1−		5
		1	15×	
2−	1−		2÷	
	3	2÷		2÷
5+		2−		

188

2÷	4−	2−	1−	
			2÷	10×
7+		40×		
2−				
8×			2−	

189

6+	2÷		2−	
	1	1−		40×
1−	2−			
	10×		3−	
12+			2÷	

190

2÷		10+		12×
15×	4			
	2÷		4−	
2−		1−		1−
1−		2÷		

191

3−	2−	2÷	20×	
			2	2−
40×		2−		
	6+			2÷
2−		1−		

192

1−	1−	4−		20×
		7+		
2÷			8+	
4−	24×			7+
	2−			

193

10+		2−	16×	
	3			
1−		80×	1	2−
2÷			60×	
		1		

194

3−	15×	1−		3−
		2÷		
3−	2÷	10+	1−	
			2−	10×
1−				

24×	2−	4−		2÷
		2÷		
	6+		2−	
4−		24×		9+
	1−			

5	4−	2÷	6×	
3−			1−	
	2	9+		10+
1−				
1−			3−	

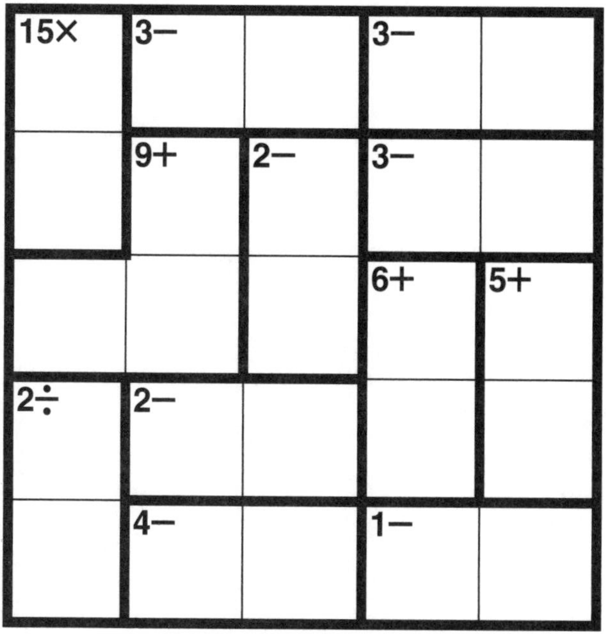

197

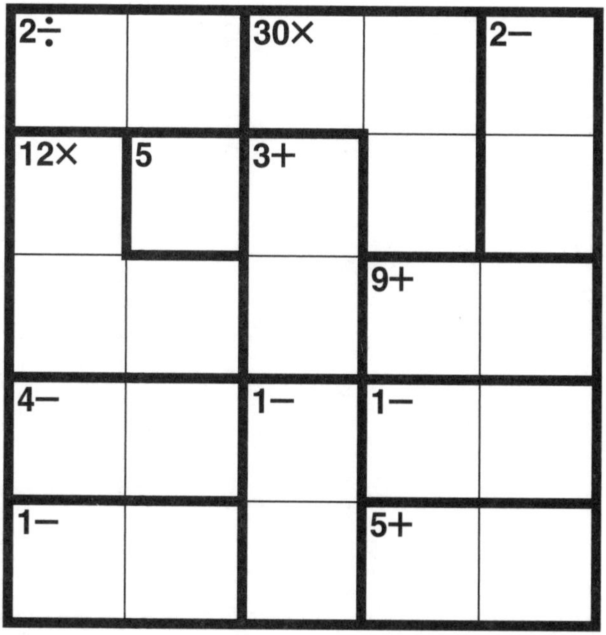

198

199

2−	3	5+	2÷	
	9+		2−	
3−		2	2−	
	30×		2−	1−
3+				

200

80×	20×		7+	
		4		4−
	12+	2÷		
		1−		40×
	2÷			

201

3−	5−	2÷	4−		1−
			2÷		
1−		3+		2÷	
3+		270×	24×		8+
6			3−		
7+			3−		

202

3+		1−	120×		
3÷			15×		5−
9+	2−		10×		
	14+		3	3−	2÷
3÷	14+		5−		
				1−	

30×	3÷		1−	5−	5
	12×				3+
	11+		3÷		
4	10×		3÷		7+
6×		2−	6×	120×	

4	4−	2÷	1−	3÷	
2÷				30×	
	2−		5−	2÷	1−
3+		36×			
20×				9×	
3÷		1−			1

13+			5−		15×
2÷		7+			
	13+	8+		2−	
4−		5−		120×	
			1−		
2	3−		14+		

5−	12×	3+		1−	
		288×		30×	
6+				6×	
60×		3÷			6
	10+		1−	5−	3−
4−					

Puzzle 207 (6×6 grid):

6+	2−		2−		72×
	5+		11+	5−	
2÷	2÷				
	13+			6+	
540×		4×		3−	
			1−		2

Puzzle 208 (6×6 grid):

3÷	50×		13+		3−
		3+	3÷		
12×	2−			30×	
		2÷	7+		30×
	1			8×	
2−		2−			

209

11+		5−		10×	
	11+			5−	
11+		10+		3÷	2÷
	9+		2		
2÷			72×		5
	30×			2÷	

210

5−	3÷	1−		32×	
		10+			
3−	1−		2÷		11+
	5−		2÷	18×	
2−		1−			3÷
2÷			6		

109

2
1
1

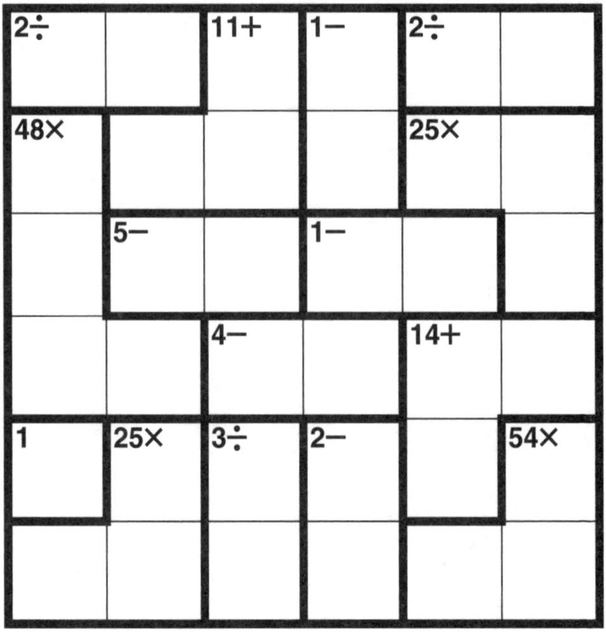
2÷
11+
1−
2÷
48×
25×
5−
1−
4−
14+
1
25×
3÷
2−
54×

2
1
2

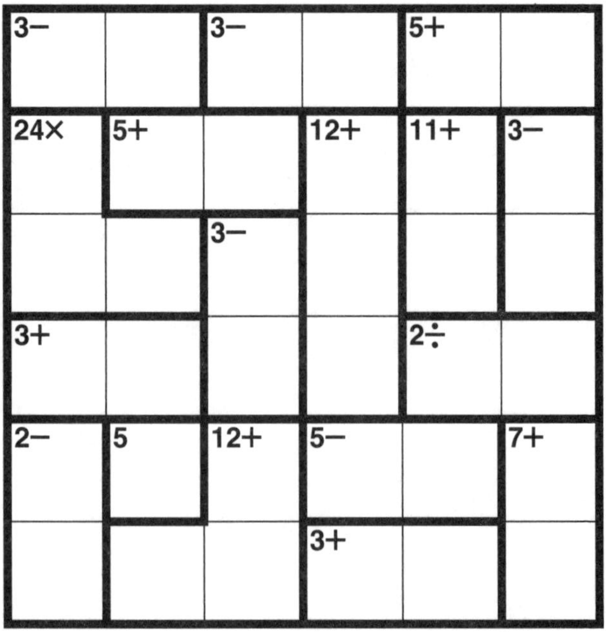
3−
3−
5+
24×
5+
12+
11+
3−
3−
3+
2÷
2−
5
12+
5−
7+
3+

Puzzle 2 1 3

1−		11+		16×	
2−		2	5−		
11+	3−	7+		20×	
		6+		11+	
5−		15+			3
			1	2÷	

Puzzle 2 1 4

48×			19+		1
6×		7+			2÷
11+			5−		
	2÷	3+		8+	
9+		80×			11+
		6			

215

2−	5−		60×		
	60×	5	5+		
3÷		3÷	1−	3−	
				6	14+
80×	3÷		5−		
				2÷	

216

3−		3÷		144×	
2÷	2÷		1−		
	9+		96×	3÷	3
3÷		5			8+
1−		5−			
5+			2−		

Puzzle 217:

90×		2÷		4	5−
		12+	11+		
5−			20×		5+
20×			1	9+	
3−	3÷	2÷			
		2−		2÷	

Puzzle 218:

1−		300×		2−	2÷
2−	4−				
		3+		2÷	
12+	3÷		4	6+	
		5−		9+	
3+		14+			

2−	32×	7+		3	16+
			24×	3+	
2÷		11+			
3+			2−		
9+	2−		5−		5+
	5−		2−		

5	3÷	36×		2÷	
20×		4		2÷	11+
		8+			
2÷		11+		3−	1−
1−			5−		
36×				1−	

Puzzle 1

12×	3÷		60×		
		3−	5−		1−
11+	2−		5+		
		7+			6
4	2÷		9+	4−	
2÷				30×	

Puzzle 2

96×		15×			1−
	11+	3+	2÷	5−	
9+					1−
	1−		14+	9+	
	60×				3−
2÷					

Puzzle 223

120×			3+		14+
2−		3	15×		
18×	20×			2÷	
		11+			2
2÷	5−		1−	240×	
	1−				

Puzzle 224

3−	2−		5−		2−
	2÷		2÷	12×	
11+		3−			
2÷			4−		2−
3÷	14+		6×		
		5−		10×	

225

3+	1−		5−	1−	
	90×	5+		3−	
			13+		2÷
2÷	10×		2÷		
	4−			36×	
2÷		30×		1	

226

2−		3+	2÷	2÷	
1−	5−			3÷	4−
		20×			
3÷	9+		2÷	3÷	
	11+			13+	
3+		3	1−		

36×			11+	2÷	1−
5−	12+				
			15×		3+
9+		15+			
2÷		5		2÷	
10×		5−		1−	

2÷		3+	90×		
3÷			9+	2−	5−
3÷	9+				
	11+			2÷	9+
6+	1−	2÷	5−		
				2÷	

Top puzzle (6×6)

5+		3−		540×	
24×		5+			
5−		17+	3÷		2
			11+		
3−			5−		8×
11+		7+			

Bottom puzzle (6×6)

5−	10×		60×	6×	
				11+	1−
5+		3÷			
2−	2−		18×		
	2−		5−	7+	
10+				5+	

Top puzzle (6×6)

2÷		3−		16×	
3−		3÷			36×
5−	9+				
	1−		11+		36×
2	4−		2÷		
24×				2−	

Bottom puzzle (6×6)

5−	3−		3+	12×	
	2−			12+	
120×			36×		12+
2÷					
72×	2÷		1−		5+
		4	6+		

KenKen Puzzle — Top Grid

1−	15×		11+		
	2÷		11+		2÷
11+	6×		12×		
	3÷	300×		12×	1−
4					
3−				2÷	

2 3 3

KenKen Puzzle — Bottom Grid

40×	1−		19+		
		10+		6+	
15+					3÷
3÷		14+	3−		
	3		11+	40×	
4−					

2 3 4

2÷	1−		3+	5−	
	6×			15+	
8+		2−			3÷
4−		5+	3÷		
2÷	5−		15+		2
		11+			

2÷		3÷	6+		15×
11+	3÷		24×		
		20×		5−	
2÷			24×	2÷	7+
1−	90×				
			7+		

120×			6+		
5−	2−		2÷	15×	
	6+	30×		11+	
4			5+		12+
2÷				5−	
30×					

24×		11+		12×	3÷
	3−	10+			
11+		4			13+
	15×		2÷		
2÷	108×			10+	3−

Top puzzle (6×6):

5−	11+		2−	2÷	
	2÷			15×	
12×		8+			5−
10+	5+	2÷	3÷		
			2÷	3−	9+
	4−				

Bottom puzzle (6×6):

360×				2÷	
9+	11+		5−	5+	
		11+		20×	1−
	4				
2÷		4	14+		
2÷		3÷		1−	

2
3
9

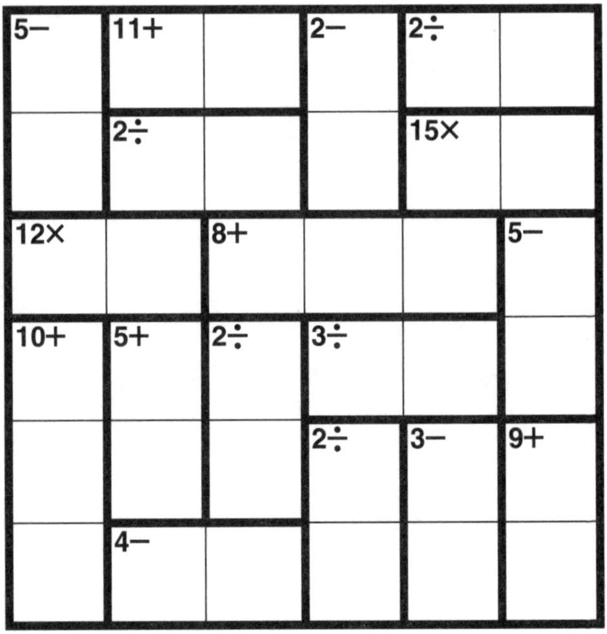

2
4
0

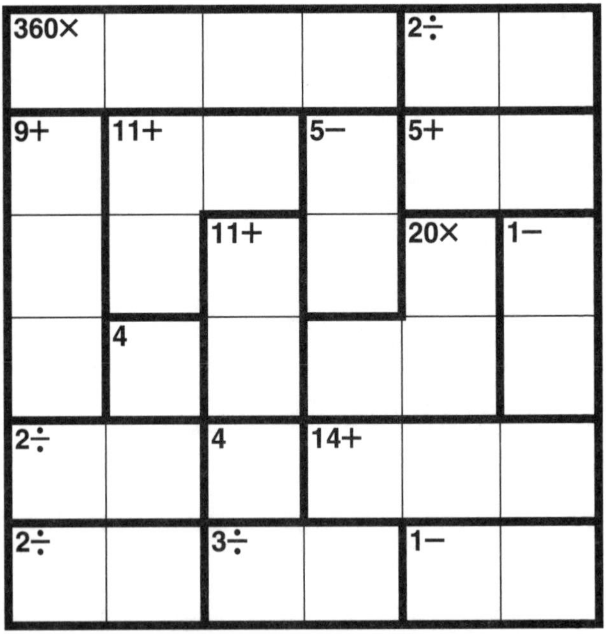

Puzzle 241

8×	3−	12+	3÷		11+
			5−		
5−			7+		1−
20×		3+		15+	
3÷	3÷				5+
	2÷		7+		

Puzzle 242

200×		7+	12×		12×
			1−	5−	
72×		5			
3÷		7+	11+	16×	
					1−
1−		10×			

Puzzle 243

5−	3+	1−	20×		10×
			2÷		
15×	12+			3+	2÷
	60×	4−			
2÷		5−	1−	4−	
				10+	

Puzzle 244

5+		2−		3÷	
24×			5−		2−
2−	5	7+			
	2÷	6+	6+		
3−			24×		15+
	5−				

Puzzle 245

11+	1−	3÷		40×	3−
		4−	2÷		
2÷	7+				2−
		20×	6+		
2−	1−		2÷	2÷	
		1		3÷	

Puzzle 246

4−		1−		25×	
20×	3+	6×	5−		
			2−	1−	
3÷	15×	11+		3÷	
			10×	3÷	2÷
2−					

Top grid (6×6):

5−	144×	20×		2−	
				20×	
2−		6	3−		
3+		7+	13+		
20×			1	3−	
2÷		3+		1−	

Bottom grid (6×6):

3	3÷		4−	240×	
11+	3÷	2÷			
			12×		
2−		8+	3	2÷	
2÷	5		15+		1−
	11+				

36×		5+		6+	2÷
120×		2−	5−		
			1−		
2÷	11+		72×		
	3÷	16×			1−
4			8+		

36×		2−		24×	1−
	3+				
14+	7+		3÷		9+
		5−		7+	
5−	40×		3		
		3+		2−	

8×	7+		7+	30×	4
					3÷
11+		4−	7+		
3+			2−		15×
2÷	24×			2÷	
	2−		5		

30×	3÷		12+		6
		5+	8+		7+
11+					
3÷	11+		2−	1−	
	32×	2		2−	6+
		3−			

Puzzle 253

3÷	3÷		2−	2÷	
	1−			5−	
120×	7+	5+		11+	5+
		2÷			
		10+	5−	5+	2−
4−					

Puzzle 254

3÷	10×	5−	1−		12×
			5−	8+	
3−	6×				20×
	2÷		2−		
2−		13+	3		
			3+		6

255

1−	3+	80×		2÷	11+
		3+			
30×			3+	7+	
9+		3−		7+	4
2−			2÷		2×
	1−				

256

8×	18×		11+		1−
			2÷	1	
5−		11+		7+	1−
2−	4				
	240×			8+	5−
2		3−			

257

1−		2−	144×	5−	
5−				3−	
120×		3+		2	4−
	6×			7+	
2÷		120×	4−		4
				2÷	

258

1−		5−	3÷	3÷	
36×	2−			20×	
		1−			9+
	30×		3+		
3−	4×	4	1−		
			8+		6

3÷		48×	6+	2−	
11+	1−			4−	
			90×		10+
3+		1−			
3−		5−		30×	
2−					3

50×		5−		10+	5+
3÷		2÷			
	12×		3+	3−	
		2÷		540×	
24×			4−		
	15×		2−		

Puzzle 261

45×		3÷	2−		3−
5			3+		
5−		1−		3−	
2÷	2−	6+		30×	
		2−			2÷
7+		30×			

Puzzle 262

1−	3÷		11+	48×	
	40×			3×	
5−		60×			
	8×			1−	
3−		6	30×		
1−		6+			4

2 / 6 / 3

48×		8+	11+		30×
			3+		
45×				2÷	6
	5−		2−		9+
15+	20×				
			3	3−	

2 / 6 / 4

20×	5+		6	1−	
		3÷	6×		
11+			9+	24×	
1−		5+		11+	
4−					5−
3÷		11+			

3÷	10+	3+		45×	
		10×			2−
9+		13+		3+	
2−			7+		13+
15×					
	10×		24×		

2÷		30×		5−	
20×	5−	11+		3+	12×
			2÷		
2−	15×	3+		240×	
			12+		
3÷					5

2−		3÷		3÷	5+
120×		2	5−		
3		1−		240×	
3+			13+		
3÷				2	2−
	1	120×			

3−	4−		2÷		3−
	24×	48×			
5				5−	7+
2÷	11+	6+	2		
			2−	1−	5−
2−					

Puzzle 269

120×		11+	2÷		3×
2−					
	6×	1−	5−	2÷	
				5	11+
2÷		2÷	216×		
5−			5		

Puzzle 270

288×			3−	2÷	
5−				30×	
9+		3÷		24×	
1−		5−			11+
15×	2÷	2−		8+	
		11+			

2÷		11+		5−	3÷
360×		2÷			
		3	8+		
3÷	3−		11+		11+
	2÷	5−			
6		2−		2−	

5−	5	2÷		48×	2−
	3÷				
9+	5+	11+	8+		4−
			2÷		
	10+	20×		5−	
		3−		5+	

10×			15+		9+
2−	20×				
	3÷			3+	15×
45×	3+	10+			
		12×	2−		5−
			10×		

1−	10×	3−		4−	
		3+	1−	10+	1
11+					2−
2÷		15+	2÷		
2÷			3−	2−	
	3−			2÷	

5−		2−	2−		10+
100×			2÷	1−	
	4	18+			
3+				5−	
	9+		3−	2÷	
3−				20×	

3÷	11+	3−	3	2÷	
			3−	2−	
2÷		10×		3−	
2−			11+	5−	2−
3×	1−				
		3÷		9+	

Puzzle 277

10×		5−	11+		2÷
2÷				2−	
20×		3+			2÷
5+		7+		14+	
	36×				9+
3÷			6+		

Puzzle 278

20×		2÷		2÷	
6+		80×	6×		5−
3÷	2÷			1−	
		11+			1−
1−	18×	10×			
			60×		

Puzzle 279

3÷		7+	40×		
2−			3÷	2	3−
5−	1−			72×	
	30×				
3−	2−	32×		10+	
			5−		

Puzzle 280

24×	11+		2÷	60×	
		7+			72×
75×			1		
24×			5−		
	10+			5−	
	5−		60×		

281

16×		2−		1	48×
	2−		4−	2÷	
11+	5+	4			
		9+	3÷		3
3÷			2÷	1−	6+
	2÷				

282

5−		1−		18×	
40×			2÷		2÷
4	10×	13+		5−	
					11+
1−	14+		3−		
		2÷		1−	

13+	5−		6×	3−	4
					15×
11+	7+	10×			
		3−		3÷	
2÷	30×	1−		2÷	
			24×		

3÷	100×		6	3+	2÷
		2÷			
12+		4	6+	12+	
	2÷			48×	
		11+			
10+			5−		

285

286

3−		18×	11+	5+	5−
13+					
	2−	9+			2÷
		3+		3−	
6+	1	48×	1−		90×

12×	1−		11+	5−	
	2÷			1−	5
18+	4	15×	2÷		1−
				9+	
	4−	18×			3÷
2			1−		

Puzzle 289

30×		3+	10+	4	36×
13+					
	30×			4−	2
2÷		12×	2÷		30×
1	11+		9+		

Puzzle 290

15×		4−		3−	
11+	12+		8×		1−
		2÷	3+		
11+				20×	
	2÷		360×	2÷	
2÷					5

1	2÷		3−	30×	
24×	2−	7+			6×
			1−		
3+		2÷		12×	3÷
1−			2×		
3−				1−	

5−		10×		1−	
1−	11+	3÷		10×	
		8×			1−
4−	2	14+	2÷		
	24×			2÷	2−
		11+			

293

2÷		10+		72×	
6	4−				24×
20×		11+	5−	2÷	
1−	36×				
		2÷	1−	11+	
				4−	

294

50×	3	2−		2÷	
		1−		5−	
5−		15+		2÷	
3÷	5−				12×
	32×	3÷	12+		
				15×	

295

3÷		6+		12×	
8+	120×	2÷	8+		5−
			16×		
		17+	11+		5
2÷				5−	6×
2−					

296

3÷	10×		24×	5−	
	2−			40×	
16+		3+			2−
12+		5−	1−		
			15×	4	3÷
	12×				

297

11+	16×	5+		2−	
			2÷	2−	
20×				3÷	
6×	18×		2÷		120×
	6		8+		
3÷		1−			

298

3−	4−		2÷		12×
	2÷	2÷	5−		
2÷			12+		3−
	2−		4−		
60×		2÷		2−	5−
			2		

Puzzle 299

2−	11+		5+		16×
	3−		2÷		
80×		2−	3÷		
	6×			1−	
3÷		24×	1−		45×

Puzzle 300

4−	24×		11+		
	3		1−		8+
5+	11+				
	2÷	10×	11+	1−	5−
15×					
	3÷		12+		

1

2 **2**	12× **3**	**4**	3− **1**
2÷ **1**	**2**	3 **3**	**4**
7+ **3**	3− **4**	**1**	1− **2**
4	3+ **1**	**2**	**3**

2

7+ **3**	**4**	3+ **1**	**2**
3+ **2**	**1**	3 **3**	3− **4**
3− **4**	1− **3**	**2**	**1**
1	2 **2**	7+ **4**	**3**

3

10+ **4**	**3**	6+ **2**	1− **1**
3	3− **1**	**4**	**2**
3+ **2**	**4**	4+ **1**	7+ **3**
1	2 **2**	**3**	**4**

4

3+ **1**	**2**	10+ **3**	**4**
2− **2**	3− **1**	**4**	**3**
4	2− **3**	**1**	5+ **2**
7+ **3**	**4**	**2**	**1**

5

6+ **2**	7+ **4**	**3**	2− **1**
4	2 **2**	3− **1**	**3**
4+ **1**	**3**	**4**	2− **2**
3 **3**	3+ **1**	**2**	**4**

6

2÷ **2**	**1**	12× **3**	4× **4**
3 **3**	6× **2**	**4**	**1**
4× **4**	**3**	2÷ **1**	**2**
1	2÷ **4**	**2**	3 **3**

7

2÷ **1**	**2**	12× **4**	**3**
2÷ **4**	3 **3**	12× **1**	2÷ **2**
2	**4**	**3**	**1**
3× **3**	**1**	8× **2**	**4**

8

12× **4**	**3**	24× **2**	2÷ **1**
2÷ **1**	4× **4**	**3**	**2**
2	**1**	**4**	12× **3**
3 **3**	2÷ **2**	**1**	**4**

9

12× 4	3	2÷ 2	1
2÷ 2	4 4	3× 1	3
1	6× 2	3	2÷ 4
3 3	4× 1	4	2

10

4 4	3+ 2	1	4+ 3
2÷ 2	4	6× 3	1
2− 1	3 3	2	2÷ 4
3	3− 1	4	2

11

4+ 3	3− 4	1	2÷ 2
1	1− 2	3	4
6× 2	3	3− 4	1
3− 4	1	5+ 2	3

12

2÷ 2	1	48× 4	3 3
2− 1	2 2	3	4
3	3− 4	1	2÷ 2
7+ 4	3	2 2	1

13

3+ 2	7+ 3	4	1 1
1	2 2	2− 3	2÷ 4
1− 3	4	1	2
3− 4	1	6× 2	3

14

6+ 1	6× 3	2	7+ 4
3	3− 4	1	2
2	1	12× 4	4+ 3
2÷ 4	2	3	1

15

2÷ 2	3− 1	4	2− 3
4	1− 3	2	1
12× 1	4	3 3	2÷ 2
3	3+ 2	1	4

16

2 2	3− 1	1− 4	3
4+ 3	4	6× 2	3− 1
1	24× 2	3	4
4	3	2÷ 1	2

156

17

36× 4	3	2÷ 1	2
3	2÷ 2	4	1 (1)
3− 1	4	1− 2	3
3+ 2	1	1− 3	4

18

2÷ 1	12× 4	3	2 (2)
2	8+ 3	6+ 4	1
3	2	1	9+ 4
3− 4	1	2	3

19

2÷ 1	2	36× 3	4
9+ 2	2− 1	3− 4	3
4	3	1	2÷ 2
3	2÷ 4	2	1

20

2÷ 4	2 (2)	4+ 1	3
2	12× 4	3	3− 1
7+ 3	2÷ 1	2	4
1	3	2− 4	2

21

6× 3	3− 1	4	2÷ 2
2	7+ 3	8+ 1	4
3− 1	4	2	2− 3
4	2	3	1

22

9+ 3	2	4	3− 1
1 (1)	6× 3	2	4
2÷ 2	4	1	8+ 3
5+ 4	1	3	2

23

8× 4	2	1	1− 3
1− 2	3− 1	3 (3)	4
3	4	9+ 2	2÷ 1
1 (1)	3	4	2

24

2÷ 1	7+ 4	3	1− 2
2	8× 1	4	3
1− 3	2	2÷ 1	3− 4
4	3 (3)	2	1

157

25

1−		6+	2÷
3	**2**	**1**	**4**
12×			
1	**4**	**3**	**2**
2÷			3
4	**1**	**2**	**3**
		3−	
2	**3**	**4**	**1**

26

3−	24×		
1	**4**	**2**	**3**
	7+	2÷	
4	**3**	**1**	**2**
12×			4
2	**1**	**3**	**4**
		5+	
3	**2**	**4**	**1**

27

1−		8×	1
2	**3**	**4**	**1**
1−	4		
3	**4**	**1**	**2**
	2÷	12+	
4	**1**	**2**	**3**
1			
1	**2**	**3**	**4**

28

2	12×		
2	**3**	**4**	**1**
9+		3	24×
1	**4**	**3**	**2**
	1	2÷	
4	**1**	**2**	**3**
1−			
3	**2**	**1**	**4**

29

3	3−		2÷
3	**1**	**4**	**2**
9+			
4	**3**	**2**	**1**
8×		2−	
2	**4**	**1**	**3**
	2	1−	
1	**2**	**3**	**4**

30

6+	12×		
2	**1**	**3**	**4**
	9+	2÷	
1	**3**	**4**	**2**
			2−
3	**4**	**2**	**1**
2÷		1	
4	**2**	**1**	**3**

31

3+		48×	
2	**1**	**3**	**4**
8+	2		
3	**2**	**4**	**1**
	2÷		1−
1	**4**	**2**	**3**
	2−		
4	**3**	**1**	**2**

32

6+			1−
3	**2**	**1**	**4**
4	5+	12×	
4	**1**	**2**	**3**
2÷			
1	**4**	**3**	**2**
	1−		1
2	**3**	**4**	**1**

33

2÷ 2	4	2− 3	3− 1
6× 3	2	1	4
6+ 1	1− 3	4	1− 2
4	1	2 2	3

34

12× 4	1	3	9+ 2
2÷ 2	4 4	1	3
1	1− 3	2	4
3 3	8× 2	4	1

35

6+ 1	1− 3	2	2÷ 4
3	16× 4	1	2
2	8× 1	4	4+ 3
4	2	3 3	1

36

4+ 1	2	1− 4	3
24× 3	1	2÷ 2	4
4	3 3	12× 1	1− 2
2	4	3	1

37

7+ 3	4	12× 1	2÷ 2
2 2	3	4	1
2÷ 1	2	1− 3	1− 4
5+ 4	1	2	3

38

1− 4	6× 3	2÷ 2	1
3	2	3− 1	4
7+ 2	3− 1	4	1− 3
1	4	3 3	2

39

12× 3	2÷ 2	1	3− 4
4	1− 3	2	1
5+ 1	4	12× 3	1− 2
1− 2	1	4	3

40

7+ 3	4	8× 1	2
2÷ 1	2	4	12× 3
2− 4	8+ 3	2	1
2	1 1	3	4

24× 3	1− 1	2÷ 4	2
4	2	7+ 3	3− 1
2	3	1	4
3− 1	4	1− 2	3

12× 3	9+ 1	2	4
4	6× 3	1	2
2÷ 1	2	12× 4	3
2	1− 4	3	1

2÷ 2	1 1	36× 4	3
4	3	1	7+ 2
2÷ 1	2	1− 3	4
1− 3	4	2	1

2÷ 1	24× 2	1− 3	4
2	3	4	1 1
9+ 4	1	1− 2	3
3 3	4	2÷ 1	2

24× 2	4	3	1 1
3 3	1	2÷ 2	4
8+ 4	1− 2	1	1− 3
1	3	4 4	2

8× 2	3− 4	1	12+ 3
1	3	2	4
4	8+ 1	3	2÷ 2
1− 3	2	4	1

8+ 1	2÷ 4	1− 2	3
4	2	3 3	8× 1
3	6× 1	5+ 4	2
2	3	1	4

2÷ 4	2÷ 2	1	2− 3
2	12× 3	4	1
3 3	6+ 1	1− 2	2÷ 4
1	4	3	2

49

4+ 1	3	2÷ 2	4
1− 3	4	1 1	1− 2
2− 2	2÷ 1	12× 4	3
4	2	3	1 1

50

1 1	2÷ 2	4	12× 3
10+ 2	3	1	4
4	1	1− 3	2
7+ 3	4	2÷ 2	1

51

7+ 2	5	8+ 3	5+ 1	4
1− 4	3	5	6+ 2	4− 1
4+ 3	6+ 2	3+ 1	4	5
1	4	2	5 5	5+ 3
4− 5	1	7+ 4	3	2

52

1− 4	3+ 2	1	3 3	4− 5
3	11+ 5	2	4	1
8+ 5	3	7+ 4	1	5+ 2
3− 1	4	5 5	2	3
3+ 2	1	8+ 3	5	4 4

53

8+ 3	1	5 5	6+ 2	4
9+ 5	4	3+ 2	1	3 3
4	2 2	8+ 3	4− 5	1
6+ 2	3	1	4	3− 5
1	9+ 5	4	3 3	2

54

9+ 5	2 2	7+ 3	1	5+ 4
4	9+ 5	3+ 2	3	1
5+ 2	4	1	8+ 5	3
3	4− 1	5	2− 4	3− 2
4+ 1	3	4 4	2	5

55

15× 5	3	2÷ 4	2	3× 1
2÷ 2	4	5× 1	5	3
12× 3	5 5	2÷ 2	1	40× 4
1	2÷ 2	45× 3	4 4	5
4	1	5	3	2

56

2÷ 2	4	20× 5	3× 3	2× 1
3× 3	15× 5	4	1	2
1	3	6× 2	20× 5	4
20× 4	1	3	2÷ 2	15× 5
5	2÷ 2	1	4	3

57

4× 4	15× 5	3	2÷ 1	2
1	3 _3_	20× 5	2	12× 4
60× 5	4	2	3	1
3	2÷ 2	1	80× 4	15× 5
2÷ 2	1	4	5	3

58

3× 3	1	80× 4	5	2÷ 2
2÷ 2	15× 3	5	4	1
1	5 _5_	6× 2	12× 3	4
20× 4	2÷ 2	3	2÷ 1	15× 5
5	4	1 _1_	2	3

59

3+ 1	2	30× 5	3	9+ 4
2÷ 4	4+ 3	2	4− 1	5
2	1	4 _4_	5	6+ 3
8+ 5	4 _4_	9+ 3	2	1
3	4− 5	1	4	2

60

40× 2	1− 3	2÷ 4	4− 5	1
5	4	2	1 _1_	18× 3
4	4− 5	1	3	2
4+ 3	1	5 _5_	11+ 2	4
3+ 1	2	12× 3	4	5

61

60× 4	4− 1	6× 3	2	5 _5_
3	5	2÷ 2	1	2÷ 4
5	12× 3	1	4	2
2÷ 2	9+ 4	5	4+ 3	1
1	6+ 2	4	15× 5	3

62

1− 3	4	2÷ 2	4− 5	1
2− 5	3	1	2÷ 4	2 _2_
3− 4	3+ 1	9+ 5	2	45× 3
1	2	4	3	5
3− 2	5	3 _3_	3− 1	4

63

2÷ 2	4− 5	1	1− 3	4
4	6× 1	3	14+ 5	2 _2_
1	2	5	4	10+ 3
11+ 5	3	2÷ 4	2	1
3	2÷ 4	2	1	5

64

2− 3	5	2÷ 1	2	40× 4
9+ 4	12× 1	3	5	2
5	2÷ 2	4	9+ 1	2− 3
2÷ 1	4	2 _2_	3	5
2	15× 3	5	4	1

65

1−4	3	10×5	2	10+1
2−5	3+1	2	3	4
3	5 5	16×4	1	2
2÷1	24×2	3	4	2−5
2	4	4−1	5	3

66

4−5	1	11+3	4	2
2÷4	15×3	5	2	2−1
2	3−5	7+4	4−1	3
8+3	2	1	5	20×4
1	4	2	3 3	5

67

12×1	3	2÷2	4	40×5
4	4−1	2−3	5	2
30×3	5	2÷1	2	4
5	2÷2	4	7+1	3
2	9+4	5	3	1 1

68

1−2	3	3+1	20×4	5
9+4	3−5	2	4+3	1
5	2	8+3	4−1	2÷4
2−3	1	4	5	2
1	4	1−5	5+2	3

69

4−1	9+5	4	6×3	2
5	1−3	2÷2	1	12+4
2÷4	2	1	5	3
2	36×1	3	2÷4	4−5
3	4	5 5	2	1

70

2÷2	9+4	2−3	4−1	5
4	5	1	15×3	1−2
2÷1	2	24×4	5	3
2−5	3	2	3−4	1
3	1 1	40×5	2	4

71

100×4	5	2 2	6+3	1
5	1−3	4	1 1	2
2÷2	4	9+1	5	3
3 3	4−1	5	2−2	4
2÷1	2	60×3	4	5

72

5 5	6×3	1	2÷4	2
2−3	5	2	1	12+4
3+1	2	4 4	3	5
2÷4	4−1	5	1−2	3
2	12×4	3	4−5	1

73

4	3+		120×	
4	**1**	**2**	**5**	**3**
11+	4−			
3	**5**	**1**	**4**	**2**
		4	2÷	
5	**3**	**4**	**2**	**1**
2÷		9+		1−
2	**4**	**3**	**1**	**5**
3+			3	
1	**2**	**5**	**3**	**4**

74

3+		1−		4+
2	**1**	**4**	**5**	**3**
4	3−		1−	
4	**2**	**5**	**3**	**1**
12×				9+
3	**4**	**1**	**2**	**5**
4−	3	2÷		
5	**3**	**2**	**1**	**4**
	8+		2÷	
1	**5**	**3**	**4**	**2**

75

15×		2÷		1−
5	**3**	**1**	**2**	**4**
4	4−	24×		
4	**1**	**2**	**3**	**5**
6+			4−	5+
2	**5**	**4**	**1**	**3**
	2−	8+		
1	**4**	**3**	**5**	**2**
			3−	
3	**2**	**5**	**4**	**1**

76

2÷	10×		1−	
2	**5**	**1**	**4**	**3**
		13+		5+
4	**2**	**3**	**5**	**1**
4+			2÷	
1	**3**	**5**	**2**	**4**
8+	2−			10×
3	**4**	**2**	**1**	**5**
	8+			
5	**1**	**4**	**3**	**2**

77

4−	9+		6×	
1	**4**	**5**	**2**	**3**
	2−		12×	
5	**2**	**4**	**3**	**1**
1−		2÷	9+	
2	**3**	**1**	**5**	**4**
12×	4−			7+
3	**1**	**2**	**4**	**5**
		4+		
4	**5**	**3**	**1**	**2**

78

3−	6×		2	2−
4	**1**	**3**	**2**	**5**
		1−		
1	**2**	**4**	**5**	**3**
8+		2÷		4
3	**5**	**2**	**1**	**4**
9+		4−	24×	
5	**4**	**1**	**3**	**2**
1−				
2	**3**	**5**	**4**	**1**

79

12×		11+	4−	
3	**2**	**4**	**5**	**1**
	8+		5+	
2	**3**	**5**	**1**	**4**
			3	30×
4	**1**	**2**	**3**	**5**
4−	5+			
5	**4**	**1**	**2**	**3**
	2−		2÷	
1	**5**	**3**	**4**	**2**

80

10×		4−	11+	
5	**2**	**1**	**4**	**3**
2÷	30×		1	
2	**3**	**5**	**1**	**4**
			2−	
4	**5**	**2**	**3**	**1**
2−	5+	2−		3−
1	**4**	**3**	**5**	**2**
		2÷		
3	**1**	**4**	**2**	**5**

164

8/1

2÷		2−		4−
4	2	5	3	1
30× 2	**6×** 3	**3−** 4	1	5
5	1	2	**9+** 4	**3** 3
3	**5+** 4	1	5	**2÷** 2
15× 1	5	3	**2** 2	4

8/2

12×		30×		
1	4	3	5	2
3	**8×** 1	4	2	**9+** 5
2÷ 2	**3−** 5	**4−** 1	**9×** 3	4
4	2	5	1	3
10+ 5	3	2	**5+** 4	1

8/3

15×		3+		20×
3	5	2	1	4
1	**12×** 4	3	**2** 2	5
1− 4	3	**4−** 1	5	**9+** 2
3− 2	**4−** 1	5	4	3
5	**2÷** 2	4	**2−** 3	1

8/4

1−		10×	4+	9+
3	2	5	1	4
60× 1	4	2	3	5
5	3	**2÷** 4	2	**1** 1
2÷ 2	**10+** 5	1	4	**10+** 3
4	**4+** 1	3	5	2

8/5

2÷		30×	2−	
4	2	5	1	3
3+ 1	3	2	**4** 4	**9+** 5
2	**2−** 1	3	**9+** 5	4
8+ 5	**1−** 4	1	3	**5+** 2
3	5	**4** 4	2	1

8/6

4−		48×	30×	
5	1	4	3	2
5+ 2	4	3	5	1
3 3	**2÷** 2	1	**1−** 4	5
3− 4	**30×** 5	2	**4+** 1	3
1	3	**7+** 5	2	**4** 4

8/7

1−		2÷	4−	
2	3	4	1	5
6+ 1	5	2	**60×** 3	4
12× 4	**2÷** 2	**8+** 3	5	**1** 1
3	1	5	**9+** 4	2
20× 5	4	**3+** 1	2	3

8/8

3−		1−		4−
2	5	3	4	1
12× 3	**3+** 2	**2÷** 4	**4−** 1	5
4	1	2	5	**3** 3
6+ 1	**7+** 3	**5** 5	**2−** 2	4
5	4	**6+** 1	3	2

165

89

4 (3−)	3 (2−)	5	1 (2÷)	2
1	2 (3+)	3 (12×)	4 (1−)	5
2 (2)	1	4	5 (30×)	3
3 (8+)	5 (8+)	1	2	4 (12×)
5	4 (4)	2	3	1

90

4 (12×)	3	1	2 (11+)	5
1 (6+)	5 (5)	3 (12×)	4	2 (3+)
5	2 (6×)	4	3 (2−)	1
3	1	2 (2)	5	4 (1−)
2 (2÷)	4	5 (4−)	1	3

91

5 (4−)	1	4 (16×)	2 (1−)	3
2 (11+)	4	1	3 (8+)	5 (4−)
4	2	3	5	1
1 (9+)	3 (2−)	5	4 (2÷)	2
3	5	2 (2)	1 (3−)	4

92

1 (2−)	3	4 (4)	5 (3−)	2
2 (2÷)	5 (5)	1 (6+)	3 (1−)	4
4	2 (3+)	5	1 (4+)	3
3 (2−)	1	2 (16×)	4	5 (4−)
5	4 (1−)	3	2	1

93

3 (2−)	1	4 (40×)	2	5
2 (2÷)	5 (30×)	3	4 (5+)	1
4	2	1 (4−)	5	3 (72×)
1 (15×)	4 (9+)	5	3	2
5	3	2 (3+)	1	4

94

5 (4−)	2 (3+)	1	4 (2÷)	3 (1−)
1	5 (60×)	3	2	4
4 (72×)	1	5 (8+)	3 (1−)	2
3	4	2	1	5 (4−)
2	3	4 (9+)	5	1

95

5 (9+)	4	1 (4−)	2 (1−)	3
2 (2÷)	3 (6×)	5	4 (3−)	1
4	1	2 (10+)	3	5 (9+)
1	2	3 (1−)	5	4
3 (15×)	5	4	1 (1−)	2

96

2 (2÷)	4	5 (15×)	3	1 (7+)
1 (4−)	5	3 (6×)	2	4
4 (1−)	3 (3)	2	1 (5+)	5 (30×)
5	2 (2÷)	1	4	3
3 (3)	1	4 (1−)	5	2

97

2÷ 4	2− 5	3	1− 1	2
2	60× 4	5	3	9+ 1
7+ 1	3	2	4× 4	5
15× 5	1	2÷ 4	2	3
3	2÷ 2	1	9+ 5	4

98

2− 3	3+ 1	60× 4	11+ 5	2
1	2	3	4	4− 5
40× 4	1− 3	5	2× 2	1
5	4	2÷ 2	1	36× 3
2	6+ 5	1	3	4

99

2− 4	2	4+ 1	3	4− 5
90× 2	3	9+ 5	4	1
3	5	2÷ 2	1	11+ 4
4− 1	12× 4	3	5	2
5	3− 1	4	1− 2	3

100

5 5	2÷ 2	1	1− 3	3− 4
2÷ 2	2− 3	50× 5	4	1
4	1	2	5	6+ 3
2− 3	20× 5	4	1	2
1	9+ 4	3	2	5 5

101

8× 4	2÷ 1	2	8+ 5	3
1	2	11+ 5	3	2÷ 4
300× 5	4	3	2÷ 1	2
5+ 3	5	9+ 4	2	4− 1
2	3	1	4	5

102

2− 5	3	3+ 1	2	1− 4
6+ 2	1	20× 5	4	3
3	2÷ 4	2	25× 1	5
2− 4	2	3 3	5	2÷ 1
4− 1	5	12× 4	3	2

103

15× 5	3	3+ 2	1	11+ 4
2÷ 2	4− 5	1	4	3
4	4+ 1	3	8+ 5	10× 2
3+ 1	2	40× 4	3	5
1− 3	4	5	2	1

104

1− 5	3− 2	5+ 1	4	3 3
4	5	1− 2	4+ 3	1
2÷ 2	4	3	4− 1	5
9× 3	4− 1	5	8+ 2	4
1	3	9+ 4	5	2

105

30× 2	3	5	9+ 4	2− 1
3− 5	2	4	1	3
7+ 4	4− 5	3+ 1	3| 3	2÷ 2
3	1	2	50× 5	4
12× 1	4	3	2	5

106

2− 3	2÷ 2	20× 5	4	2− 1
5	4	2÷ 2	1	3
2÷ 2	4− 5	1	60× 3	4
4	3× 1	7+ 3	5	3− 2
1	3	4	2	2	5

107

12× 4	3− 5	2− 3	1	3+ 2
3	2	10× 5	7+ 4	1
5| 5	1	2	3	9+ 4
2÷ 1	1− 3	2÷ 4	2	5
2	4	4− 1	5	3| 3

108

1− 3	4	4− 1	5	8× 2
30× 5	3	2	1| 1	4
3+ 2	20× 5	4	12+ 3	1
1	2÷ 2	5	4	15× 3
4| 4	1	5+ 3	2	5

109

20× 4	1	1	4− 5	7+ 3	1− 2
5	2	1	4	3
2÷ 1	3	40× 4	2	5
2	2− 5	3	4− 1	5+ 4
12× 3	4	2	2	5	1

110

2÷ 2	1	2− 3	5	48× 4
15× 5	5+ 4	1	2	3
3	9+ 5	4	3− 1	2
1	1− 3	2	4	4− 5
11+ 4	2	5	3| 3	1

111

12× 3	4	4− 1	10+ 2	5	5
2÷ 4	30× 2	5	3	1
2	5	4+ 3	1	4
6+ 1	3	11+ 4	5	2
5	3+ 1	2	1− 4	3

112

3− 1	4	6× 3	2	4− 5
2− 4	2	5| 5	12+ 3	1
1− 3	4− 1	2÷ 2	5	4
2	5	4	2− 1	3
2− 5	3	3− 1	4	2| 2

168

113

9+ 5	4	12× 1	7+ 3	2
2÷ 4	4− 1	3	2	2− 5
2	5	4	5+ 1	3
18× 3	2	7+ 5	4	1
1	3	2	1− 5	4

114

7+ 1	60× 4	5	1− 2	3
4	2	3	4− 5	1
4− 5	1	2÷ 2	1− 3	4
90× 2	3	1	9+ 4	5
3	5	3− 4	1	2 2

115

10× 2	3+ 1	1− 4	3	60× 5
5	2	4− 1	4	3
4+ 1	3	5	3+ 2	4 4
1− 4	2− 5	3	1	8+ 2
3	2÷ 4	2	5	1

116

6× 3	2	4− 1	5	12+ 4
9+ 4	3+ 1	2	3	5
5	1− 4	7+ 3	8+ 1	2
2÷ 1	5	4	2	3
2	15× 3	5	3− 4	1

117

4− 5	1	2÷ 4	1− 2	3
2÷ 4	5 5	2	4+ 3	6+ 1
2	24× 4	3	1	5
7+ 3	2	4− 1	1− 5	4
1	3	5	2÷ 4	2

118

24× 2	3	9+ 5	4	2÷ 1
4	4− 1	15× 3	5	2
4− 1	5	1− 2	3	12× 4
5	7+ 2	4	1	3
1− 3	4	1	3− 2	5

119

1− 4	1− 3	4− 1	5	2÷ 2
3	2	20× 5	4	1
10× 2	9+ 4	4+ 3	1	2− 5
1	5	4	1− 2	3
5	3+ 1	2	3	4 4

120

2÷ 2	1− 4	3	4− 5	1
4	10× 2	5	12× 1	3
3 3	1	2÷ 2	4	9+ 5
8+ 5	3	1	12× 2	4
4− 1	5	4 4	3	2

121

4− 5	1	2÷ 2	4 4	6× 3
8+ 3	3− 5	4	2	1
4	2	12+ 1	3	5
1	4 4	3	10× 5	2
30× 2	3	5	1	4 4

122

3 3	6+ 1	4	50× 5	2
13+ 4	3	1	3+ 2	5
10× 5	4	2	1	8+ 3
2	2− 5	3	4	1
2÷ 1	2	60× 5	3	4

123

1− 3	4− 1	5	2÷ 4	2
4	15× 5	3	6× 2	1
3− 5	10+ 2	1	3	4 4
2	3	2÷ 4	4− 1	2− 5
1	4	2	5	3

124

1− 3	9+ 5	4	10× 2	1
4	3× 1	3	5	2 2
2÷ 2	4	1	11+ 3	5
1− 1	2	9+ 5	4	3
15× 5	3	2 2	5+ 1	4

125

2÷ 2	4	4− 5	1	12× 3
1− 5	1− 3	2	4	1
4	3+ 2	1	6× 3	9+ 5
2− 1	15× 5	3	2	4
3	1	3− 4	5	3− 2

126

9+ 5	4+ 3	1	24× 2	4
4	2÷ 1	2	3	5 5
10× 1	2	5	24× 4	3
1− 3	60× 5	4	1	2
2	4 4	3	4− 5	1

127

2 2	2÷ 4	2− 1	3	1− 5
9+ 5	2	45× 3	2÷ 1	4
4	3	5	2	6× 1
4− 1	5	2÷ 2	20× 4	3
2− 3	1	4	5	2

128

1− 2	3	4− 5	8× 4	3− 1
3 3	3− 5	1	2	4
5+ 1	2	1− 4	5	8+ 3
4	2÷ 1	2	6× 3	5
9+ 5	4	3 3	1	2

129

3+ 1	2	36× 3	4− 4	5
2÷ 2	20× 4	5	3	1
4	30× 5	6× 1	2	3
2− 5	3	2	10+ 1	4
3	5+ 1	4	5	2² 2

130

5+ 4	4+ 1	3	10× 2	5
1	12+ 4	5	3	2÷ 2
10+ 5	1− 3	2	4− 1	4
3	2÷ 2	4	5	4+ 1
2	5 5	5+ 1	4	3

131

1 1	2− 2	4	3	5
2÷ 2	4	3 3	20× 5	4+ 1
12+ 5	3+ 1	2	4	3
3	4− 5	1	8+ 2	4
4	2− 3	5	1 1	2

132

2÷ 2	4	1	4− 5	15× 3
15× 3	3+ 2	7+ 4	1	5
5	1	3	2÷ 4	2
1	12+ 5	3− 2	1− 3	4
4	3	5	2÷ 2	1

133

4− 1	5	2− 3	8× 2	4
2÷ 2	4	5	36× 3	1
1− 5	2÷ 2	1	4	3
4	11+ 3	3+ 2	1	50× 5
3	1	4	5	2

134

2− 5	3	2÷ 4	2	1 1
3+ 2	1− 5	12× 1	3	4
1	4	40× 2	5	1− 3
12× 3	4− 1	5	4	2
4	5+ 2	3	4− 1	5

135

4+ 3	1− 2	1	20× 4	5
1	2− 5	3	2÷ 2	4
15+ 5	4	2	1	3
6+ 2	3 3	4	15× 5	2÷ 1
4	4− 1	5	3	2

136

4 4	2÷ 1	2	2− 5	3
3+ 2	1− 3	4− 1	1− 4	5
1	2	5	6× 3	5+ 4
8+ 3	1− 5	4	2	1
5	7+ 4	3	2÷ 1	2

137

2÷	60×		2÷	
1	**3**	**5**	**2**	**4**
2	**4**	**3** (13+)	**5**	**1**
3 (4+)	**1**	**2** (2−)	**4**	**5** (10+)
5 (200×)	**2**	**4**	**1** (4+)	**3**
4	**5**	**1** (1)	**3**	**2**

138

4−	15×	1−	2÷	
5	**3**	**4**	**1**	**2**
1	**5**	**3**	**2** (3−)	**4** (12×)
4 (4)	**1** (3+)	**2**	**5**	**3**
2 (48×)	**4**	**1** (4−)	**3** (2−)	**5**
3	**2**	**5**	**4** (3−)	**1**

139

6×	20×	7+		7+
2	**5**	**4**	**3**	**1**
3	**4**	**2** (2÷)	**1**	**5**
4 (60×)	**3**	**1**	**5** (5)	**2** (2÷)
5	**1** (4+)	**3** (2−)	**2** (9+)	**4**
1	**2**	**5**	**4**	**3**

140

9+		6×		6+
5	**4**	**2**	**3**	**1**
2 (2÷)	**1**	**3**	**4**	**5**
1 (2−)	**2** (10×)	**4** (20×)	**5**	**3** (1−)
3	**5**	**1** (4−)	**2** (4×)	**4**
4 (1−)	**3**	**5**	**1**	**2**

141

15×	3+		1−	4
3	**2**	**1**	**5**	**4**
1	**5**	**3** (3)	**4**	**2** (10×)
4 (5+)	**1**	**2** (6×)	**3**	**5**
5 (3−)	**3**	**4** (2÷)	**2**	**1** (4+)
2	**4**	**5** (4−)	**1**	**3**

142

4+		2−	2÷	
1	**3**	**5**	**4**	**2**
2 (30×)	**5**	**3**	**1** (3−)	**4**
3	**2** (2÷)	**4**	**5** (4−)	**1**
4 (20×)	**1** (3−)	**2** (1−)	**3**	**5** (2−)
5	**4**	**1** (2÷)	**2**	**3**

143

9+		10×		12×
4	**5**	**2**	**1**	**3**
2 (2÷)	**1**	**5**	**3** (6×)	**4**
5 (4−)	**3** (48×)	**4**	**2**	**1**
1	**4**	**3** (10+)	**5**	**2**
3 (3)	**2** (2÷)	**1**	**4** (1−)	**5**

144

1−	3−	9+	1−	
1	**4**	**5**	**3**	**2**
2	**1**	**4**	**5** (2−)	**3**
4 (2÷)	**2**	**3** (30×)	**1** (4−)	**5**
3 (8+)	**5**	**2**	**4** (16×)	**1**
5	**3** (3)	**1** (1−)	**2**	**4**

Puzzle 145

3− 4	6× 3	1	12+ 5	2
1	2	1− 3	4	5
10+ 3	4− 1	5	24× 2	4
5	2÷ 4	2	3× 1	3
2	9+ 5	4	3	1

Puzzle 146

2÷ 1	40× 4	2	5	2− 3
2	3 3	15× 5	2÷ 4	1
9+ 5	1	3	2	4 4
4	2÷ 2	1	3 3	7+ 5
2− 3	5	5+ 4	1	2

Puzzle 147

18× 3	4− 5	1	7+ 2	1− 4
2	3	4	1	5
2÷ 4	2	45× 5	3	30× 1
3− 1	4	3	5	2
4− 5	1	2÷ 2	4	3

Puzzle 148

2÷ 2	1	20× 5	4	10+ 3
1	1− 4	3	4− 5	2
3 3	2− 2	4	1	5
1− 5	8+ 3	2÷ 1	2÷ 2	4
4	5	2	4+ 3	1

Puzzle 149

2÷ 4	6× 2	3	2− 1	9+ 5
2	2− 5	3− 1	3	4
4− 5	3	4	2÷ 2	1
1	2÷ 4	2	5	2− 3
3 3	4− 1	5	2− 4	2

Puzzle 150

3× 3	1	9+ 4	5	10+ 2
1	2− 4	2	3	5
2÷ 4	2	4− 5	1	12× 3
10+ 5	3	15× 1	2÷ 2	4
2	5	3	4	1

Puzzle 151

40× 5	3 3	15× 1	2− 4	2
4	2	3	6+ 1	5
1− 3	4	5	2÷ 2	1
3+ 2	1	1− 4	5	3 3
4− 1	5	2 2	1− 3	4

Puzzle 152

60× 4	1− 2	3	3+ 1	4− 5
3	5	5+ 4	2	1
4− 5	1− 3	1	2÷ 4	2
1	4	3− 2	2− 5	3
2÷ 2	1	5	1− 3	4

2÷ 1	2	2÷ 4	2− 5	3
6+ 5	1	2	1− 3	4
40× 2	3 3	20× 5	4	1
4	5	2− 3	1	3− 2
12× 3	4	2÷ 1	2	5

1− 3	2÷ 2	2− 1	1− 4	5
4	1	3	50× 5	2− 2
2− 1	3	5	2	4
7+ 2	9+ 5	1− 4	3	2− 1
5	4	2÷ 2	1	3

9+ 4	5	2− 1	24× 3	2
3− 5	5+ 1	3	2÷ 2	4
2	4	1− 5	1	15× 3
5+ 3	2	4	5	1
4+ 1	3	40× 2	4	5

48× 3	4	5	1	2÷ 2
4	2÷ 2	2− 3	5	1
8+ 5	1	8× 2	10+ 3	4 4
1	15× 3	4	2	5
2	5	1	1− 4	3

10× 2	4− 5	1− 4	3	2− 1
5	1	2÷ 2	4	3
2÷ 1	2	11+ 3	4− 5	40× 4
4 4	3	5	1	2
1− 3	4	1− 1	2	5

15× 5	2÷ 2	1− 3	4	2÷ 1
3	4	6+ 5	1	2
6+ 1	3	2	1− 5	4
2÷ 2	1	5+ 4	1− 3	2− 5
9+ 4	5	1	2	3

2÷ 2	2− 3	1	2− 5	1− 4
4	1− 1	2 2	3	5
5 5	2	12× 3	4	2− 1
2− 1	4 4	7+ 5	2	3
3	9+ 5	4	2÷ 1	2

1− 4	4− 1	5	18× 2	3
5	13+ 4	2	3	5+ 1
2	5	2− 3	1	4
2− 3	2÷ 2	1	1− 4	5
1	12× 3	4	3− 5	2

161

4+		60×	2÷	
1	3	5	4	2
3−				1−
4	1	3	2	5
30×	1−		6+	
3	5	2	1	4
		7+		3
2	4	1	5	3
			4+	
5	2	4	3	1

162

15×		2−		10+
5	3	4	2	1
9+		8+		
3	2	5	1	4
	1		90×	
4	1	2	3	5
2÷	60×			
1	4	3	5	2
		3−		
2	5	1	4	3

163

10×		7+	2−	1−
2	5	4	1	3
4−				
5	1	2	3	4
	5+	2−	2−	5
1	2	3	4	5
11+				2÷
4	3	5	2	1
		6+		
3	4	1	5	2

164

2−	3+		1−	
3	2	1	4	5
	12×	2	2−	2÷
5	1	2	3	4
12+				
1	3	4	5	2
		1−		2−
4	5	3	2	1
	4	4−		
2	4	5	1	3

165

3+		20×		2−
2	1	4	5	3
7+		2÷		
4	3	1	2	5
9+	1−		12×	
5	2	3	1	4
	1−			2÷
1	4	5	3	2
	3−		4	
3	5	2	4	1

166

9+		6×		1
4	5	2	3	1
1−	2÷		9+	1−
3	2	1	5	4
2	4	3	1	5
4−	2−		2÷	
1	3	5	4	2
	3−		1−	
5	1	4	2	3

167

4−	9+		1−	
1	4	5	2	3
	6×			2÷
5	3	2	1	4
10+		8+		
3	5	1	4	2
2÷			4−	
4	2	3	5	1
		3−		2−
2	1	4	3	5

168

10+	2−		30×	
4	3	1	2	5
	2÷			9+
5	1	2	3	4
	32×		4−	
1	2	4	5	3
1−		2−		
3	4	5	1	2
	5		3−	
2	5	3	4	1

169

40× 5	1	2	1− 3	4
3+ 1	4	3− 5	2	8+ 3
2	2− 3	1	1− 4	5
24× 3	2	4	5	2÷ 1
20× 4	5	4+ 3	1	2

170

2− 4	2	2− 3	4− 5	1
3− 2	5	1	1− 3	4
5+ 1	4	5 5	24× 2	3
12+ 5	3	4	1	7+ 2
3 3	2÷ 1	2	4	5

171

2− 3	1	1− 4	50× 2	5
30× 1	4 4	3	5	2÷ 2
5	6+ 2	1	3	4
2	3	20× 5	4	1
11+ 4	5	2	2− 1	3

172

1− 2	3	1	4− 5	5+ 4
2− 3	5	8× 2	4	1
2÷ 4	2	5 5	1	1− 3
4− 5	5+ 1	1− 4	30× 3	2
1	4	3	2	5

173

4− 1	5	2÷ 4	2	2− 3
2− 2	30× 3	5	1− 4	1
4	1	2	3	9+ 5
2− 3	9+ 2	4− 1	5	4
5	4	3	2÷ 1	2

174

2÷ 4	2	2− 3	1	11+ 5
6+ 1	20× 4	5	30× 3	2
3	1 1	2	5	4
2	20× 5	1	9+ 4	3
2− 5	3	4	2	1 1

175

6× 1	3	2	9+ 4	5
1− 2	4− 1	2− 3	5	2÷ 4
3	5	12× 4	1	2
1− 4	2÷ 2	4− 5	3	6+ 1
5	4	1	2	3

176

3+ 2	12× 4	1	3 3	11+ 5
1	4− 5	3	1− 4	2
1− 3	1	9+ 2	5	4
4	2	5	2− 1	3
12+ 5	3	4	2÷ 2	1

177

11+		3+		48×
3	**5**	**2**	**1**	**4**
2	**1**	**5** (12+)	**4**	**3**
5 (10+)	**4**	**3**	**2** (3−)	**1** (2÷)
4	**3** (6×)	**1**	**5**	**2**
1	**2**	**4** (1−)	**3**	**5** (5)

178

4−	1−	40×		2−
5	**3**	**4**	**2**	**1**
1	**2**	**5**	**4** (5+)	**3**
3 (15×)	**5**	**2** (2÷)	**1**	**4** (9+)
2 (2÷)	**4** (8+)	**1**	**3** (10+)	**5**
4	**1**	**3**	**5**	**2**

179

11+	4−		12×	1−
2	**5**	**1**	**3**	**4**
3	**2**	**4**	**1**	**5**
4	**3** (2−)	**5** (10×)	**2**	**1**
5 (4−)	**1**	**2** (2÷)	**4**	**3** (1−)
1	**4** (4)	**3** (15×)	**5**	**2**

180

3−		12×		
5	**2**	**4**	**1**	**3**
2 (1−)	**5** (1−)	**1** (15×)	**3** (7+)	**4**
1	**4**	**3**	**5**	**2** (2÷)
4 (7+)	**3** (2−)	**5**	**2** (2÷)	**1**
3	**1** (2÷)	**2**	**4**	**5** (5)

181

90×		5+		1−
2	**3**	**4**	**1**	**5**
3	**5**	**1** (4−)	**2** (1−)	**4**
4 (40×)	**2**	**5**	**3**	**1** (2−)
5	**1** (2÷)	**2**	**4** (14+)	**3**
1 (5+)	**4**	**3**	**5**	**2**

182

16×	2÷		2−	
4	**1**	**2**	**5**	**3**
1	**4**	**5** (9+)	**3**	**2** (2÷)
5 (10+)	**2** (2)	**3** (12×)	**1**	**4**
2	**3** (2−)	**1**	**4**	**5** (4−)
3	**5**	**4** (2÷)	**2**	**1**

183

2−		2−		40×
1	**3**	**2**	**4**	**5**
3 (1−)	**5** (9+)	**1** (4−)	**2**	**4**
2	**4**	**5**	**3** (4+)	**1**
5 (1−)	**2** (2÷)	**4** (4)	**1** (15×)	**3** (1−)
4	**1**	**3**	**5**	**2**

184

40×		1−	7+	
1	**5**	**2**	**4**	**3**
2	**4**	**3**	**5** (4−)	**1**
5 (120×)	**2**	**1** (2−)	**3**	**4** (4)
3	**1** (10+)	**4** (2÷)	**2**	**5** (7+)
4	**3**	**5**	**1**	**2**

185

60× 4	2− 1	3	3− 2	5
3	5	8+ 4	1	3+ 2
3− 2	9+ 4	5	3	1
5	6× 2	2÷ 1	1− 4	1− 3
1 1	3	2	5	4

186

4− 5	1	16× 2	8+ 3	4
8+ 3	2	4	1	4− 5
2	3	1− 5	4	1
3− 4	1− 5	2÷ 1	2	1− 3
1	4	2− 3	5	2

187

2− 2	2÷ 1	1− 3	4	5 5
4	2	1 1	15× 5	3
2− 3	1− 5	4	2÷ 2	1
5	3 3	2÷ 2	1	2÷ 4
5+ 1	4	2− 5	3	2

188

2÷ 2	4− 5	2− 1	1− 3	4
4	1	3	2÷ 2	10× 5
7+ 3	4	40× 5	1	2
2− 5	3	2	4	1
8× 1	2	4	2− 5	3

189

6+ 1	2÷ 4	2	2− 5	3
5	1 1	1− 4	3	40× 2
1− 2	2− 3	1	4	5
3	10× 2	5	3− 1	4
12+ 4	5	3	2÷ 2	1

190

2÷ 2	1	10+ 3	5	12× 4
15× 5	4 4	2	3	1
3	2÷ 2	4	4− 1	5
2− 1	3	1− 5	4	1− 2
1− 4	5	2÷ 1	2	3

191

3− 1	2− 3	2÷ 2	20× 4	5
4	5	1	2 2	2− 3
40× 2	4	2− 5	3	1
5	6+ 2	3	1	2÷ 4
2− 3	1	1− 4	5	2

192

1− 3	1− 2	4− 5	1	20× 4
4	3	7+ 1	2	5
2÷ 2	1	4	8+ 5	3
4− 5	24× 4	2	3	7+ 1
1	5	2− 3	4	2

193

10+ 5	1	**2−** 3	**16×** 4	2
4	**3** 3	5	2	1
1− 3	4	**80×** 2	**1** 1	**2−** 5
2÷ 1	2	4	**60×** 5	3
2	5	**1** 1	3	4

194

3− 2	**15×** 5	**1−** 3	4	**3−** 1
5	3	**2÷** 2	1	4
3− 4	**2÷** 1	**10+** 5	**1−** 2	3
1	2	4	**2−** 3	**10×** 5
1− 3	4	1	5	2

195

24× 4	**2−** 3	**4−** 5	1	**2÷** 2
3	5	**2÷** 4	2	1
2	**6+** 4	1	**2−** 5	3
4− 5	1	**24×** 2	3	**9+** 4
1	2	3	4	5

196

5 5	**4−** 1	**2÷** 4	**6×** 2	3
3− 4	5	2	**1−** 3	1
1	**2** 2	**9+** 3	4	**10+** 5
1− 2	3	5	1	4
1− 3	4	1	**3−** 5	2

197

15× 3	**3−** 1	4	**3−** 2	5
5	**9+** 2	**2−** 3	**3−** 4	1
4	3	5	**6+** 1	**5+** 2
2÷ 1	**2−** 4	2	5	3
2	**4−** 5	1	**1−** 3	4

198

2÷ 2	4	**30×** 3	5	**2−** 1
12× 4	**5** 5	**3+** 1	2	3
1	3	2	**9+** 4	5
4− 5	1	**1−** 4	**1−** 3	2
1− 3	2	5	**5+** 1	4

199

2− 5	**3** 3	**5+** 4	**2÷** 2	1
3	**9+** 5	1	**2−** 4	2
3− 1	4	**2** 2	**2−** 5	3
4	**30×** 2	3	**2−** 1	**1−** 5
3+ 2	1	5	3	4

200

80× 2	**20×** 4	5	**7+** 1	3
5	2	**4** 4	3	**4−** 1
4	**12+** 3	**2÷** 1	2	5
1	5	**1−** 3	4	**40×** 2
3	**2÷** 1	2	5	4

201

3− 2	5− 6	2÷ 4	4− 1	5	1− 3
5	1	2	2÷ 3	6	4
1− 4	5	3+ 1	2	2÷ 3	6
3+ 1	2	270× 3	24× 6	4	8+ 5
6 6	3	5	3− 4	1	2
7+ 3	4	6	3− 5	2	1

202

3+ 2	1	1− 3	120× 4	6	5
3÷ 6	2	4	15× 5	3	5− 1
9+ 4	2− 3	1	10× 2	5	6
5	14+ 6	2	3 3	3− 1	2÷ 4
3÷ 3	14+ 5	6	5− 1	4	2
1	4	5	6	1− 2	3

203

30× 3	3÷ 6	2	1− 4	5− 1	5 5
2	12× 3	4	5	6	3+ 1
5	11+ 4	6	3÷ 1	3	2
4 4	10× 5	1	3÷ 6	2	7+ 3
6× 6	1	2− 3	6× 2	120× 5	4
1	2	5	3	4	6

204

4 4	4− 5	2÷ 1	1− 3	3÷ 6	2
2÷ 3	1	2	4	30× 5	6
6	2− 3	5	5− 1	2÷ 2	1− 4
3+ 1	2	36× 3	6	4	5
20× 5	4	6	2	9× 1	3
3÷ 2	6	1− 4	5	3	1 1

205

13+ 4	5	2	5− 6	1	15× 3
2÷ 6	2	7+ 3	4	5	1
3	13+ 6	8+ 5	1	2− 4	2
4− 5	3	5− 1	2	6	120× 4
1	4	6	1− 3	2	5
2 2	3− 1	4	14+ 5	3	6

206

5− 6	12× 3	3+ 2	1	1− 4	5
1	4	288× 6	2	30× 5	3
6+ 5	1	4	6	6× 3	2
60× 4	5	3÷ 1	3	2	6 6
3	10+ 2	5	1− 4	5− 6	3− 1
4− 2	6	3	5	1	4

207

6+ 1	2− 3	5	2− 2	4	72× 6
5	5+ 2	3	11+ 6	5− 1	4
2÷ 4	2÷ 1	2	5	6	3
2	13+ 4	6	3	6+ 5	1
540× 3	6	4× 4	1	3− 2	5
6	5	1	1− 4	3	2 2

208

3÷ 6	50× 2	5	13+ 4	3	3− 1
2	5	3+ 1	3÷ 3	6	4
12× 4	2− 6	2	1	30× 5	3
1	4	2÷ 3	7+ 5	2	30× 6
3	1 1	6	2	8× 4	5
2− 5	3	2− 4	6	1	2

209

11+	5−		10×		
3	4	6	1	5	2
4	11+ 2	3	5	5− 6	1
11+ 5	1	10+ 2	4	3÷ 3	2÷ 6
6	9+ 5	4	2 2	1	3
2÷ 2	3	1	72× 6	4	5 5
1	30× 6	5	3	2÷ 2	4

210

5−	3÷	1−		32×	
1	3	6	5	4	2
6	1	10+ 2	3	5	4
3− 5	1− 4	3	2÷ 1	2	11+ 6
2	5− 6	1	2÷ 4	18× 3	5
2− 3	5	1− 4	2	6	3÷ 1
2÷ 4	2	5	6 6	1	3

211

2÷		11+	1−	2÷	
6	3	4	5	1	2
48× 2	4	3	6	25× 5	1
4	5− 6	1	1− 3	2	5
3	2	4− 5	1	14+ 6	4
1 1	25× 5	3÷ 6	2− 2	4	54× 3
5	1	2	4	3	6

212

3−		3−		5+	
6	3	5	2	4	1
24× 1	5+ 2	3	12+ 4	11+ 6	3− 5
4	6	3− 1	3	5	2
3+ 2	1	4	5	2÷ 3	6
2− 3	5 5	12+ 2	5− 6	1	7+ 4
5	4	6	3+ 1	2	3

213

1−		11+		16×	
2	3	6	5	4	1
2− 3	5	2 2	5− 6	1	4
11+ 6	3− 1	7+ 3	4	20× 2	5
5	4	6+ 1	3	11+ 6	2
5− 1	6	15+ 4	2	5	3 3
4	2	5	1 1	2÷ 3	6

214

48×			19+		1
4	6	2	3	5	1
6× 2	1	7+ 3	5	6	2÷ 4
11+ 5	3	4	5− 6	1	2
6	2÷ 4	3+ 1	2	8+ 3	5
9+ 3	2	80× 5	1	4	11+ 6
1	5	6 6	4	2	3

215

2−	5−		60×		
4	6	1	5	2	3
6	60× 3	5 5	5+ 4	1	2
3÷ 3	5	3÷ 6	1− 2	3− 4	1
1	4	2	3	6 6	14+ 5
80× 2	3÷ 1	3	5− 6	5	4
5	2	4	1	2÷ 3	6

216

3−		3÷		144×	
5	2	3	1	6	4
2÷ 3	2÷ 1	2	1− 5	4	6
6	9+ 5	4	96× 2	3÷ 1	3 3
3÷ 2	6	5 5	4	3	8+ 1
1− 4	3	5− 1	6	2	5
5+ 1	4	6	2− 3	5	2

217

90×		2÷		4	5−
3	5	1	2	4	6
2	3	12+ 4	11+ 5	6	1
5− 6	1	2	20× 4	5	5+ 3
20× 5	4	6	1	9+ 3	2
3− 4	3÷ 2	2÷ 3	6	1	5
1	6	2− 5	3	2÷ 2	4

218

1−		300×		2−	2÷
2	3	4	5	6	1
2− 6	4− 1	5	3	4	2
4	5	3+ 1	2	2÷ 3	6
12+ 3	3÷ 6	2	4 4	6+ 1	5
5	4	5− 6	1	9+ 2	3
3+ 1	2	14+ 3	6	5	4

219

2−	32×	7+		3	16+
1	4	2	5	3	6
3	2	4	24× 6	3+ 1	5
2÷ 6	3	11+ 5	4	2	1
3+ 2	1	6	2− 3	5	4
9+ 4	2− 5	3	5− 1	6	5+ 2
5	5− 6	1	2− 2	4	3

220

5	3÷	36×		2÷	
5	6	3	4	2	1
20× 1	2	4 4	3	2÷ 6	11+ 5
4	5	8+ 1	2	3	6
2÷ 2	1	11+ 6	5	3− 4	1− 3
1− 3	4	5	5− 6	1	2
36× 6	3	2	1	1− 5	4

221

12×	3÷		60×		
1	2	6	5	3	4
3	4	3− 5	5− 6	1	1− 2
11+ 6	2− 5	2	5+ 1	4	3
5	3	7+ 1	4	2	6 6
4 4	2÷ 6	3	9+ 2	4− 5	1
2÷ 2	1	4	3	30× 6	5

222

96×		15×			1−
6	4	3	1	5	2
4	11+ 5	3+ 1	2÷ 2	5− 6	3
9+ 3	6	2	4	1	1− 5
1	3	4	14+ 5	9+ 2	6
5	60× 2	6	3	4	3− 1
2÷ 2	1	5	6	3	4

223

120×			3+		14+
5	6	4	2	1	3
2− 4	2	3 3	15× 1	5	6
18× 6	20× 4	5	3	2÷ 2	1
3	5	11+ 1	4	6	2 2
2÷ 2	5− 1	6	1− 5	240× 3	4
1	1− 3	2	6	4	5

224

3−	2−		5−		2−
2	3	5	1	6	4
5	2÷ 1	2	2÷ 4	12× 3	6
11+ 6	5	3− 3	2	4	1
2÷ 4	2	6	4− 5	1	2− 3
3÷ 1	14+ 6	4	6× 3	2	5
3	4	1	5− 6	10× 5	2

225

3+	1−		5−	1−	
2	**4**	**3**	**1**	**5**	**6**
	90×	5+		3−	
1	**3**	**4**	**6**	**2**	**5**
			13+		2÷
5	**6**	**1**	**3**	**4**	**2**
2÷	10×		2÷		
3	**5**	**2**	**4**	**6**	**1**
	4−			36×	
6	**1**	**5**	**2**	**3**	**4**
2÷		30×		1	
4	**2**	**6**	**5**	**1**	**3**

226

2−		3+	2÷	2÷	
5	**3**	**1**	**6**	**4**	**2**
1−	5−			3÷	4−
4	**1**	**2**	**3**	**6**	**5**
		20×			
3	**6**	**4**	**5**	**2**	**1**
3÷	9+		2÷	3÷	
6	**4**	**5**	**2**	**1**	**3**
		11+		13+	
2	**5**	**6**	**1**	**3**	**4**
3+		3	1−		
1	**2**	**3**	**4**	**5**	**6**

227

36×			11+	2÷	1−
3	**6**	**2**	**5**	**1**	**4**
5−	12+				
1	**3**	**4**	**6**	**2**	**5**
			15×		3+
6	**4**	**1**	**3**	**5**	**2**
9+		15+			
4	**5**	**3**	**2**	**6**	**1**
2÷		5		2÷	
2	**1**	**5**	**4**	**3**	**6**
10×		5−		1−	
5	**2**	**6**	**1**	**4**	**3**

228

2÷		3+		90×	
4	**2**	**1**	**5**	**6**	**3**
3÷			9+	2−	5−
3	**1**	**2**	**4**	**5**	**6**
3÷	9+				
6	**5**	**4**	**2**	**3**	**1**
	11+			2÷	9+
2	**6**	**5**	**3**	**1**	**4**
6+	1−	2÷	5−		
1	**4**	**3**	**6**	**2**	**5**
				2÷	
5	**3**	**6**	**1**	**4**	**2**

229

5+		3−		540×	
4	**1**	**2**	**5**	**6**	**3**
24×		5+			
3	**2**	**1**	**4**	**5**	**6**
5−		17+	3÷		2
6	**4**	**5**	**1**	**3**	**2**
			11+		
1	**3**	**6**	**2**	**4**	**5**
3−			5−		8×
2	**5**	**3**	**6**	**1**	**4**
11+		7+			
5	**6**	**4**	**3**	**2**	**1**

230

5−		10×		60×	6×
6	**5**	**1**	**4**	**3**	**2**
				11+	1−
1	**2**	**3**	**5**	**6**	**4**
5+		3÷			
4	**1**	**6**	**2**	**5**	**3**
2−		2−		18×	
5	**4**	**2**	**3**	**1**	**6**
		2−		5−	7+
3	**6**	**4**	**1**	**2**	**5**
10+				5+	
2	**3**	**5**	**6**	**4**	**1**

231

2÷		3−		16×	
3	**6**	**2**	**5**	**1**	**4**
3−		3÷			36×
5	**2**	**3**	**1**	**4**	**6**
5−	9+				
6	**4**	**5**	**3**	**2**	**1**
	1−		11+		36×
1	**3**	**4**	**6**	**5**	**2**
2	4−		2÷		
2	**5**	**1**	**4**	**6**	**3**
24×				2−	
4	**1**	**6**	**2**	**3**	**5**

232

5−	3−		3+	12×	
6	**5**	**2**	**1**	**3**	**4**
	2−			12+	
1	**3**	**5**	**2**	**4**	**6**
120×		36×			12+
5	**4**	**6**	**3**	**2**	**1**
2÷					
2	**1**	**3**	**4**	**6**	**5**
72×	2÷		1−		5+
4	**2**	**1**	**6**	**5**	**3**
		4	6+		
3	**6**	**4**	**5**	**1**	**2**

233

1− 2	15× 5	3	11+ 4	1	6
3	2÷ 2	4	11+ 6	5	2÷ 1
11+ 5	6× 6	1	12× 3	4	2
6	3÷ 3	300× 5	1	12× 2	1− 4
4 4	1	6	2	3	5
3− 1	4	2	5	2÷ 6	3

234

40× 5	1− 1	2	19+ 3	6	4
4	2	10+ 1	5	6+ 3	6
15+ 6	5	4	1	2	3÷ 3
3÷ 3	4	14+ 6	3− 2	5	1
1	3 3	5	11+ 6	40× 4	2
4− 2	6	3	4	1	5

235

2÷ 3	1− 4	5	3+ 2	5− 1	6
6	6× 2	3	1	15+ 4	5
8+ 5	3	2− 2	4	6	3÷ 1
4− 1	5	5+ 4	3÷ 6	2	3
2÷ 4	5− 6	1	15+ 3	5	2 2
2	1	11+ 6	5	3	4

236

2÷ 2	4	3÷ 6	6+ 1	5	15× 3
11+ 6	3÷ 1	2	24× 3	4	5
5	3	20× 4	2	5− 1	6
2÷ 1	2	5	24× 6	2÷ 3	7+ 4
1− 3	90× 5	1	4	6	2
4	6	3	7+ 5	2	1

237

120× 5	4	6	6+ 2	3	1
5− 1	2− 2	4	2÷ 6	15× 5	3
6	6+ 1	30× 2	3	11+ 4	5
4 4	5	3	5+ 1	2	12× 6
2÷ 3	6	5	4	5− 1	2
30× 2	3	1	5	6	4

238

24× 4	2	11+ 5	6	12× 1	3÷ 3
3	3− 4	10+ 2	5	6	1
11+ 5	1	4 4	3	2	13+ 6
6	15× 5	1	2÷ 2	3	4
2÷ 1	108× 6	3	4	10+ 5	3− 2
2	3	6	1	4	5

239

5− 1	11+ 6	5	2− 3	2÷ 4	2
6	2÷ 2	4	1	15× 5	3
12× 4	3	8+ 2	5	1	5− 6
10+ 5	5+ 4	2÷ 3	3÷ 6	2	1
2	1	6	2÷ 4	3− 3	9+ 5
3	4− 5	1	2	6	4

240

360× 6	5	3	4	2÷ 1	2
9+ 5	11+ 3	2	5− 6	5+ 4	1
3	6	11+ 5	1	20× 2	1− 4
1	4 4	6	2	5	3
2÷ 2	1	4 4	14+ 5	3	6
2÷ 4	2	3÷ 1	3	1− 6	5

184

241

8×	3−	12+	3÷		11+
2	**5**	**4**	**1**	**3**	**6**
4	**2**	**3**	**6** 5−	**1**	**5**
6 5−	**1**	**5**	**3** 7+	**4**	**2** 1−
5 20×	**4**	**1** 3+	**2**	**6** 15+	**3**
3 3÷	**6** 3÷	**2**	**4**	**5**	**1** 5+
1	**3** 2÷	**6**	**5** 7+	**2**	**4**

242

200×		7+	12×		12×
2	**5**	**6**	**4**	**3**	**1**
5	**4**	**1**	**2** 1−	**6** 5−	**3**
6 72×	**2**	**5** 5	**3**	**1**	**4**
1 3÷	**6**	**3** 7+	**5** 11+	**4** 16×	**2**
3	**1**	**4**	**6**	**2**	**5** 1−
4 1−	**3**	**2** 10×	**1**	**5**	**6**

243

5−	3+	1−	20×		10×
6	**1**	**3**	**5**	**4**	**2**
1	**2**	**4**	**6** 2÷	**3**	**5**
5 15×	**6** 12+	**2**	**4**	**1** 3+	**3** 2÷
3	**4** 60×	**5** 4−	**1**	**2**	**6**
4 2÷	**3**	**6** 5−	**2** 1−	**5** 4−	**1**
2	**5**	**1**	**3**	**6** 10+	**4**

244

5+		2−		3÷	
1	**4**	**3**	**5**	**6**	**2**
3 24×	**2**	**4**	**6** 5−	**1**	**5** 2−
6 2−	**5** 5	**2** 7+	**1**	**4**	**3**
4	**6** 2÷	**5** 6+	**2** 6+	**3**	**1**
5 3−	**3**	**1**	**4** 24×	**2**	**6** 15+
2	**1** 5−	**6**	**3**	**5**	**4**

245

11+	1−	3÷		40×	3−
6	**2**	**3**	**1**	**5**	**4**
5	**3**	**2** 4−	**6** 2÷	**4**	**1**
4 2÷	**1** 7+	**6**	**3**	**2**	**5** 2−
2	**6**	**4** 20×	**5** 6+	**1**	**3**
1 2−	**4** 1−	**5**	**2** 2÷	**3** 2÷	**6**
3	**5**	**1** 1	**4**	**6** 3÷	**2**

246

4−		1−		25×	
2	**6**	**4**	**3**	**5**	**1**
4 20×	**2** 3+	**3** 6×	**1** 5−	**6**	**5**
5	**1**	**2**	**6** 2−	**4** 1−	**3**
1 3÷	**3** 15×	**5** 11+	**4**	**2** 3÷	**6**
3	**5**	**6**	**2** 10×	**1** 3÷	**4** 2÷
6 2−	**4**	**1**	**5**	**3**	**2**

247

5−	144×	20×		2−	
6	**2**	**4**	**5**	**3**	**1**
1	**4**	**3**	**6**	**2** 20×	**5**
5 2−	**3**	**6** 6	**4** 3−	**1**	**2**
2 3+	**1**	**5** 7+	**3** 13+	**4**	**6**
4 20×	**5**	**2**	**1** 1	**6** 3−	**3**
3 2÷	**6**	**1** 3+	**2**	**5**	**4**

248

3	3÷		4−	240×	
3	**2**	**6**	**1**	**4**	**5**
6 11+	**1** 3÷	**2** 2÷	**5**	**3**	**4**
5	**3**	**4**	**2** 12×	**1**	**6**
4 2−	**6**	**5** 8+	**3** 3	**2** 2÷	**1**
1 2÷	**5** 5	**3**	**4** 15+	**6**	**2** 1−
2	**4** 11+	**1**	**6**	**5**	**3**

249

3 (36×)	6	1 (5+)	4	5 (6+)	2 (2÷)
5 (120×)	2	3 (2−)	6 (5−)	1	4
6	4	5	1	2 (1−)	3
2 (2÷)	5 (11+)	6	3 (72×)	4	1
1	3 (3÷)	4 (16×)	2	6	5 (1−)
4 (4)	1	2	5 (8+)	3	6

250

2 (36×)	6	3 (2−)	5	1 (24×)	4 (1−)
3	1 (3+)	2	4	6	5
5 (14+)	3 (7+)	4	6 (3÷)	2	1 (9+)
4	5	6 (5−)	1	3 (7+)	2
1 (5−)	2 (40×)	5	3 (3)	4	6
6	4	1 (3+)	2	5 (2−)	3

251

1 (8×)	5 (7+)	2	3 (7+)	6 (30×)	4 (4)
4	2	3	1	5	6 (3÷)
5 (11+)	6	1 (4−)	4 (7+)	3	2
2 (3+)	1	5	6 (2−)	4	3 (15×)
6 (2÷)	3 (24×)	4	2	1 (2÷)	5
3	4 (2−)	6	5 (5)	2	1

252

5 (30×)	1 (3÷)	3	2 (12+)	4	6 (6)
2	3	1 (5+)	5 (8+)	6	4 (7+)
6 (11+)	5	4	1	2	3
3 (3÷)	6 (11+)	5	4 (2−)	1	2 (1−)
1	4 (32×)	2 (2)	6	3 (2−)	5 (6+)
4	2	6 (3−)	3	5	1

253

6 (3÷)	3 (3÷)	1	5 (2−)	4 (2÷)	2
2	4 (1−)	5	3	1 (5−)	6
5 (120×)	1 (7+)	3 (5+)	2	6 (11+)	4 (5+)
3	6	2 (2÷)	4	5	1
4	2	6 (10+)	1 (5−)	3 (5+)	5 (2−)
1 (4−)	5	4	6	2	3

254

6 (3÷)	2 (10×)	1 (5−)	5 (1−)	4	3 (12×)
2	5	6	1 (5−)	3 (8+)	4
4 (3−)	1 (6×)	3	6	5	2 (20×)
1	3 (2÷)	2	4 (2−)	6	5
5 (2−)	6	4 (13+)	3 (3)	2	1
3	4	5	2 (3+)	1	6 (6)

255

2 (1−)	1 (3+)	4 (80×)	5	3 (2÷)	6 (11+)
3	2	1 (3+)	4	6	5
5 (30×)	6	2	1 (3+)	4 (7+)	3
1 (9+)	3	6 (3−)	2	5 (7+)	4 (4)
4 (2−)	5	3	6 (2÷)	2	1 (2×)
6	4 (1−)	5	3	1	2

256

1 (8×)	3 (18×)	2	5 (11+)	6	4 (1−)
4	2	3	6 (2÷)	1 (1)	5
6 (5−)	1	5 (11+)	3	4 (7+)	2 (1−)
5 (2−)	4 (4)	6	1	2	3
3	6 (240×)	4	2	5 (8+)	1 (5−)
2 (2)	5	1 (3−)	4	3	6

257

1− 3	4	2− 5	144× 2	5− 1	6
5− 6	1	3	4	3− 5	2
120× 4	6	3+ 1	3	2 2	4− 5
5	6× 3	2	6	7+ 4	1
2÷ 1	2	120× 6	4− 5	3	4 4
2	5	4	1	2÷ 6	3

258

1− 5	4	5− 6	3÷ 2	3÷ 3	1
36× 2	2− 3	1	6	20× 4	5
6	5	1− 3	4	1	9+ 2
3	30× 6	5	3+ 1	2	4
3− 1	4× 2	4 4	1− 5	6	3
4	1	2	3	8+ 5	6 6

259

3÷ 3	1	48× 6	6+ 5	2− 4	2
11+ 5	1− 3	4	1	4− 2	6
6	4	90× 2	3	5	10+ 1
3+ 1	2	1− 3	4	6	5
3− 2	5	5− 1	6	30× 3	4
2− 4	6	5	2	1	3 3

260

50× 5	2	5− 1	6	10+ 3	5+ 4
3÷ 2	5	2÷ 6	3	4	1
6	12× 4	3	3+ 1	3− 5	2
3	1	2÷ 4	2	540× 6	5
24× 4	6	2	4− 5	1	3
1	15× 3	5	2− 4	2	6

261

45× 3	5	3÷ 2	2− 6	4	3− 1
5 5	3	6	3+ 2	1	4
5− 6	1	1− 3	4	3− 2	5
2÷ 4	2− 6	6+ 5	1	30× 3	2
2	4	2− 1	3	5	2÷ 6
7+ 1	2	4	30× 5	6	3

262

1− 2	3÷ 3	1	11+ 5	48× 4	6
3	40× 5	4	6	3× 1	2
5− 6	2	60× 5	4	3	1
1	8× 4	2	3	1− 6	5
3− 4	1	6 6	30× 2	5	3
1− 5	6	6+ 3	1	2	4 4

263

48× 1	4	8+ 3	11+ 5	6	30× 2
2	6	4	3+ 1	5	3
45× 5	3	1	2	2÷ 4	6 6
3	5− 1	6	2− 4	2	9+ 5
15+ 4	20× 2	5	6	3	1
6	5	2	3 3	3− 1	4

264

20× 1	5+ 2	3	6 6	1− 4	5
5	4	3÷ 6	6× 2	1	3
11+ 6	5	2	9+ 1	24× 3	4
1− 4	3	5+ 1	5	11+ 6	2
4− 2	6	4	3	5	5− 1
3÷ 3	1	11+ 5	4	2	6

Grid labels (left margin): 257, 258, 259, 260, 261, 262, 263, 264

265

3÷	10+	3+		45×	
6	4	2	1	5	3
2	6	1	5	3	4
4	5	3	2	1	6
1	3	6	4	2	5
5	1	4	3	6	2
3	2	5	6	4	1

266

2÷		30×		5−	
2	4	3	5	6	1
4	6	5	2	1	3
5	1	6	3	2	4
3	5	1	6	4	2
1	3	2	4	5	6
6	2	4	1	3	5

267

2−		3÷		3÷	5+
5	3	6	2	1	4
4	5	2	6	3	1
3	6	4	1	5	2
1	2	3	5	4	6
6	4	1	3	2	5
2	1	5	4	6	3

268

3−	4−		2÷		3−
4	1	5	6	3	2
1	3	6	4	2	5
5	2	4	1	6	3
6	5	3	2	1	4
3	6	2	5	4	1
2	4	1	3	5	6

269

120×		11+	2÷		3×
6	5	3	4	2	1
5	4	6	2	1	3
3	1	5	6	4	2
2	3	4	1	5	6
4	2	1	3	6	5
1	6	2	5	3	4

270

288×			3−	2÷	
6	4	3	5	2	1
1	6	4	2	5	3
4	5	1	3	6	2
2	3	6	1	4	5
5	1	2	4	3	6
3	2	5	6	1	4

271

2÷		11+		5−	3÷
2	4	6	5	1	3
5	3	4	2	6	1
4	6	3	1	5	2
1	5	2	4	3	6
3	2	1	6	4	5
6	1	5	3	2	4

272

5−	5	2÷		48×	2−
6	5	1	2	4	3
1	6	2	4	3	5
4	1	6	3	5	2
3	4	5	1	2	6
2	3	4	5	6	1
5	2	3	6	1	4

188

273

10×			15+		9+
2	5	1	3	6	4
2− 6	**20×** 4	5	1	3	2
4	**3÷** 6	2	5	**3+** 1	**15×** 3
45× 3	**3+** 1	**10+** 6	4	2	5
5	2	**12×** 3	**2−** 6	4	**5−** 1
1	3	4	**10×** 2	5	6

274

1−	10×	3−		4−	
4	2	3	6	1	5
3	5	**3+** 2	**1−** 4	**10+** 6	**1** 1
11+ 5	6	1	3	4	**2−** 2
2÷ 6	3	**15+** 5	**2÷** 1	2	4
2÷ 1	4	6	2	**3−** 5	**2−** 3
2	1	**3−** 4	5	3	**2÷** 6

275

5−		2−	2−		10+
6	1	3	2	4	5
100× 4	5	1	**2÷** 6	**1−** 2	3
5	**4** 4	**18+** 6	3	1	2
3+ 2	3	4	5	**5−** 6	1
1	**9+** 2	5	**3−** 4	**2÷** 3	6
3− 3	6	2	1	**20×** 5	4

276

3÷	11+	3−	3	2÷	
6	5	4	3	2	1
2	6	1	**3−** 4	**2−** 5	3
2÷ 4	2	**10×** 5	1	**3−** 3	6
2− 5	3	2	**11+** 6	**5−** 1	**2−** 4
3× 1	**1−** 4	3	5	6	2
3	1	**3÷** 6	2	**9+** 4	5

277

10×		5−	11+		2÷
2	5	6	3	4	1
2÷ 3	6	1	4	**2−** 5	2
20× 5	4	**3+** 2	1	3	**2÷** 6
5+ 4	1	**7+** 5	2	**14+** 6	3
1	**36×** 3	4	6	2	**9+** 5
3÷ 6	2	3	**6+** 5	1	4

278

20×		2÷		2÷	
5	4	3	6	1	2
6+ 1	5	**80×** 4	**6×** 3	2	**5−** 6
3÷ 6	**2÷** 2	5	4	**1−** 3	1
2	1	**11+** 6	5	4	**1−** 3
1− 3	**18×** 6	**10×** 2	1	5	4
4	3	1	**60×** 2	6	5

279

3÷		7+	40×		
3	1	6	2	5	4
2− 4	6	1	**3÷** 3	**2** 2	**3−** 5
5− 6	**1−** 4	5	1	**72×** 3	2
1	**30×** 2	3	5	4	6
3− 5	**2−** 3	**32×** 2	4	**10+** 6	1
2	5	4	**5−** 6	1	3

280

24×	11+		2÷	60×	
1	6	5	4	3	2
6	4	**7+** 1	2	5	**72×** 3
75× 5	3	4	**1** 1	2	6
24× 3	5	2	**5−** 6	1	4
4	**10+** 2	3	5	**5−** 6	1
2	**5−** 1	6	**60×** 3	4	5

281

16×	2−		1	48×	
4	2	5	3	1	6
2	5	3	1	6	4
6	1	4	5	3	2
5	4	1	6	2	3
3	6	2	4	5	1
1	3	6	2	4	5

282

5−		1−		18×	
6	1	4	5	2	3
5	4	2	6	3	1
4	5	6	3	1	2
1	2	3	4	6	5
2	3	5	1	4	6
3	6	1	2	5	4

283

13+	5−		6×	3−	4
3	1	6	2	5	4
4	6	1	3	2	5
6	4	2	5	1	3
5	3	4	1	6	2
1	2	5	4	3	6
2	5	3	6	4	1

284

3÷	100×		6	3+	2÷
1	4	5	6	2	3
3	5	2	4	1	6
6	1	4	3	5	2
4	6	1	2	3	5
2	3	6	5	4	1
5	2	3	1	6	4

285

5−	75×		9+		
6	1	5	3	4	2
1	3	2	4	6	5
4	5	3	6	2	1
5	4	1	2	3	6
3	2	6	1	5	4
2	6	4	5	1	3

286

120×	11+		72×		3−
2	6	5	4	3	1
3	5	1	2	6	4
5	4	2	3	1	6
1	3	4	6	2	5
4	2	6	1	5	3
6	1	3	5	4	2

287

3−		18×	11+	5+	5−
2	5	3	6	4	1
4	3	2	5	1	6
6	4	5	1	3	2
3	6	1	2	5	4
5	1	6	4	2	3
1	2	4	3	6	5

288

12×	1−		11+	5−	
4	3	2	5	6	1
3	2	4	6	1	5
6	4	5	1	2	3
1	6	3	2	5	4
5	1	6	3	4	2
2	5	1	4	3	6

30× 5	6	3+ 2	10+ 1	4 4	36× 3
13+ 3	4	1	5	2	6
6	30× 3	5	4	4− 1	2 2
2÷ 4	2	12× 3	2÷ 6	5	30× 1
2	1	4	3	6	5
1 1	11+ 5	6	9+ 2	3	4

15× 3	5	4− 2	6	3− 4	1
11+ 6	12+ 3	5	8× 4	1	1− 2
5	4	2÷ 6	3+ 1	2	3
11+ 1	6	3	2	20× 5	4
4	2÷ 2	1	360× 5	2÷ 3	6
2÷ 2	1	4	3	6	5 5

1 1	2÷ 2	4	3− 3	30× 6	5
24× 4	2− 5	7+ 2	6	1	6× 3
6	3	5	1− 4	2	1
3+ 2	1	2÷ 3	5	12× 4	3÷ 6
1− 5	4	6	2× 1	3	2
3− 3	6	1	2	1− 5	4

5− 6	1	10× 2	5	1− 3	4
1− 4	11+ 6	3÷ 3	1	5	2
3	5	8× 1	2	4	1− 6
4− 1	2 2	14+ 4	2÷ 3	6	5
5	24× 3	6	4	2÷ 2	2− 1
2	4	11+ 5	6	1	3

2÷ 1	2	10+ 3	5	72× 4	6
6 6	4− 5	1	2	3	24× 4
20× 5	4	11+ 6	5− 1	2÷ 2	3
1− 4	36× 3	5	6	1	2
3	1	2÷ 2	1− 4	11+ 6	5
2	6	4	3	4− 5	1

50× 5	3 3	2− 4	6	2÷ 2	1
2	5	1− 3	4	5− 1	6
5− 6	1	15+ 5	3	2÷ 4	2
3÷ 3	5− 6	1	2	5	12× 4
1	32× 4	3÷ 2	12+ 5	6	3
4	2	6	1	15× 3	5

3÷ 6	2	6+ 5	1	12× 3	4
8+ 4	120× 6	2÷ 2	8+ 3	5	5− 1
3	5	1	16× 2	4	6
1	4	17+ 3	11+ 6	2	5 5
2÷ 2	1	4	5	5− 6	6× 3
2− 5	3	6	4	1	2

3÷ 3	10× 2	5	24× 4	5− 6	1
1	2− 5	3	6	40× 2	4
16+ 6	4	3+ 2	1	5	2− 3
12+ 4	6	5− 1	1− 2	3	5
5	1	6	15× 3	4 4	3÷ 2
2	12× 3	4	5	1	6

6 (11+)	**2** (16×)	**4** (5+)	**1**	**5** (2−)	**3**
5	**4**	**2** (2÷)	**6**	**3** (2−)	**1**
4 (20×)	**5**	**1**	**3**	**6** (3÷)	**2**
3 (6×)	**1** (18×)	**6**	**2** (2÷)	**4**	**5** (120×)
2	**6** (6)	**3**	**5** (8+)	**1**	**4**
1 (3÷)	**3**	**5** (1−)	**4**	**2**	**6**

2 (3−)	**1** (4−)	**5**	**3** (2÷)	**6**	**4** (12×)
5	**4** (2÷)	**2** (2÷)	**6** (5−)	**1**	**3**
6 (2÷)	**2**	**1**	**4** (12+)	**3**	**5** (3−)
3	**6** (2−)	**4**	**1** (4−)	**5**	**2**
4 (60×)	**3**	**6** (2÷)	**5**	**2** (2−)	**1** (5−)
1	**5**	**3**	**2** (2)	**4**	**6**

3 (2−)	**6** (11+)	**5**	**4** (5+)	**1**	**2** (16×)
1	**5** (3−)	**2**	**3** (2÷)	**6**	**4**
5 (80×)	**4**	**3** (2−)	**6** (3÷)	**2**	**1**
4	**3** (6×)	**1**	**2**	**5** (1−)	**6**
2 (3÷)	**1**	**6** (24×)	**5** (1−)	**4**	**3** (45×)
6	**2**	**4**	**1**	**3**	**5**

2 (4−)	**6** (24×)	**4**	**1** (11+)	**5**	**3**
6	**3** (3)	**1**	**4** (1−)	**2**	**5** (8+)
4 (5+)	**5** (11+)	**6**	**3**	**1**	**2**
1	**4** (2÷)	**2** (10×)	**5** (11+)	**3** (1−)	**6** (5−)
3 (15×)	**2**	**5**	**6**	**4**	**1**
5	**1** (3÷)	**3**	**2** (12+)	**6**	**4**